GHOSTS

Henrik Ibsen

in a version by Mike Poulton

SERVING THEATRE

SF

SINCE 1830

SAMUELFRENCH-LONDON.CO.UK
SAMUELFRENCH.COM

FOR AMATEUR PRODUCTION ENQUIRIES

UNITED KINGDOM AND WORLD EXCLUDING NORTH AMERICA
plays@SamuelFrench-London.co.uk
020 7255 4302/01

UNITED STATES AND CANADA
info@SamuelFrench.com
1-866-598-8449

Each title is subject to availability from Samuel French, depending upon country of performance.

GHOSTS

By Henrik Ibsen in a version by Mike Poulton

**First presented by Clwyd Theatr Cymru, Mold
Flintshire, Wales, 25 September 2014**

CAST

Pastor Manders	**Simon Dutton**
Osvald Alving	**Owain Gwynn**
Mrs Helen Alving	**Siân Howard**
Regina Engstrand	**Michelle Luther**
Jacob Engstrand	**Llion Williams**

CREATIVE

Director	**Emma Lucia**
Designer	**Simon Kenny**
Composer	**Colin Towns**
Lighting	**Nick Beadle**
Sound	**Matthew Williams**
Assistant Director	**Rupert Hands**

Company Stage Manager	**Paul Sawtell**
Stage Manager (on the book)	**Edward Salt**
Assistant Stage Manager	**Sara-Lee Bull**

DIRECTOR'S NOTE

GHOSTS is the most accomplished play of Ibsen's middle period. Like a thriller, the revelations rise to fever pitch. Characters tell truths, half-truths, lies - conscious and unconscious. They are the product of a religiously intolerant society reflected in their language and behaviour.

Like all Ibsen's best work, GHOSTS is a debate. It tackles religious indoctrination, familial duty, freedom of expression, sexual politics, moral and physical corruption, even euthanasia. It is unsettling and yet absorbing. When Pastor Manders asks Mrs Alving whether they may be overheard, we feel, guiltily, that he may be referring to us – the silent witnesses.

Mrs Alving struggles with the harrowing realization that her best intentions have made her a destructive conspirator. Manders' muddled brain tries to grapple with the messy realities of human existence. Osvald struggles to unearth the mysteries of his illness. Regina dreams of Paris - a distant Arcadia. And from the underworld lurks Jacob Engstrand whose satanic presence employs religious rhetoric for malign purposes.

There are ghosts everywhere. It's not just the dead who haunt Mrs Alving. It is also dead beliefs and ideals. In a metaphorical echo of the disease 'whose name they dare not speak', they are riddled with behavioural patterns that prevent their leading healthy, natural lives. Osvald gets closest to what life might be like by escaping to Paris and becoming an artist. Fleetingly he finds an alternative to a world where it seems to rain inside and out.

Like Oedipus, the more Mrs Alving questions the past the closer she moves towards her destruction. As the sun comes up for what feels like the very first time, light falls on the shadows of the past and the ghosts are finally dispelled.

Mike Poulton's adaptation provides a sparse, tense and thrilling version of the text. His bible is William Archer's English edition – authorised by Ibsen himself. Every word is chosen with exactitude. Characters speak a language that is at once familiar yet of its time. The text, like the play, crackles with energy.

Emma Lucia, September 2014

GHOSTS

Henrik Ibsen

in a version by Mike Poulton

DRAMATIS PERSONAE

MRS HELEN ALVING — a rich landowner
OSVALD ALVING — her son, an artist
PASTOR MANDERS
JAKOB ENGSTRAND — a carpenter
REGINA ENGSTRAND — his supposed daughter, brought up in the
Alving household
SERVANTS

ACT ONE

REGINA. *(coming in sees* **ENGSTRAND** *at the door)* Not in the house! Out! Out! Dripping water everywhere –

ENGSTRAND. God's good rain, Regina –

REGINA. Get out!

ENGSTRAND. Give us a chance! Listen – I'm not going no –

REGINA. Club-foot clumping about –

ENGSTRAND. Don't shove me –

REGINA. Come on, out – you'll wake Master Osvald –

ENGSTRAND. Not still in bed, is he? –

REGINA. What's it to do with you? –

ENGSTRAND. This time of day? Wait. Listen to what I've to say. Then I'll be off.

REGINA. Hurry up then –

ENGSTRAND. Not so loud! I had a few drinks last night and my head's –

REGINA. A few! Look at you!

ENGSTRAND. Nobody's perfect. Satan digs pits for the weak and frail.

REGINA. You throw yourself into all of them –

ENGSTRAND. I was at my bench at half past five this morning –

REGINA. You'll get no sympathy from me. Last thing I need's to be caught in a rendezvous with an old sot like –

ENGSTRAND. A what with a –

REGINA. I'll not have Mrs Alving think I let you in the house. So come on – out.

1

ENGSTRAND. When I've said what I came to say. *(pause)* My work at the orphanage finishes this afternoon – I'm going back to town on the last steamer –

REGINA. Good.

ENGSTRAND. Grand Opening tomorrow – the orphanage. Drink. Champagne flowing...
You know what I'm like – better not lead myself into temptation –

REGINA. Ha! –

ENGSTRAND. Mustn't disgrace myself in front of my betters. *(he studies her)*
Pastor Manders will be there –

REGINA. And he'll be here – now – any minute, so –

ENGSTRAND. I'm in Manders' good books and I want to stay in 'em.

REGINA. *(studies him)* You and Manders? What are you up to?

ENGSTRAND. Nothing – you're filling out, girl –

REGINA. Why do you need to keep the right side of Pastor Manders? What do you want out of him?

ENGSTRAND. I don't know what you mean. I want nothing from Manders. He's always been fair with me. The only one what's ever trusted me – pitied my weaknesses. Look, Regina, I'm off home tonight –

REGINA. Good riddance.

ENGSTRAND. And you're coming with me. *(pause)*

REGINA. I... I am not! *(stunned)*

ENGSTRAND. I need you back home, Regina.

REGINA. You're out of your mind. I can't believe...! When I've been brought up by a lady like Mrs Alving – treated almost like her daughter... You think I'd go... The stink of you disgusts me – ugghhh – the very idea –

ENGSTRAND. I'm your father, Regina. *(pause)*

REGINA. You've denied it – hundreds of times. I pray it's the truth.

ENGSTRAND. I can tell the truth when it suits me.

REGINA. The things you called me – ma foi!

ENGSTRAND. I don't remember calling you that –

REGINA. After what you did to me... You're evil –

ENGSTRAND. Only when I'm drunk.

Don't blame me – blame the devil what gets into me – it's a weakness, I tell you – It's in the blood, Regina.

Or blame your mother – I do. She's the one what drove me to it.

I had to get back at her, didn't I? Stuck up bitch!

Oh yes she was, Regina, working in this house for Mr and Mrs high and mighty Alving – O I beg his late lamented pardon! – King's Councillor and Mrs Alving – it changed her. It'll change you too if I let you stay here. We're all what God made us – mustn't get above ourselves –

REGINA. You drove my mother to an early grave.

ENGSTRAND. She dug it herself.

REGINA. Stop that! *(he is tapping his club foot)* Pied de mouton!

ENGSTRAND. She's taught you English then?

REGINA. *(sneers)* Mais oui! Je parle l'Anglais.

ENGSTRAND. Good. That'll come in useful.

REGINA. What do you want? Tell me and get out.

ENGSTRAND. I'm your father. What does any lonely widower want with his girl?

REGINA. You disgust me –

ENGSTRAND. I've had this idea –

REGINA. It won't work.

ENGSTRAND. It can't fail! Jesus God, when I think –

REGINA. Don't use your filthy language in this house –

ENGSTRAND. Look, I've been well paid for the work I've done on the orphanage – I'm a good carpenter – Christ's own trade – and I've got a bit put by.

REGINA. Have you? How much?

ENGSTRAND. Well there's nothing to spend it on, is there? Stuck out here in the country –

REGINA. How much?

ENGSTRAND. I want to invest it

REGINA. Invest it? You! Invest – oho!

ENGSTRAND. In a mission house. For sailor boys.

REGINA. A mission? You...? Oh, I see – you mean a whore-house.

ENGSTRAND. *(real anger)* Shut your mouth or I'll leather you! *(slight pause)* It's going to be high class lodgings – respectable – fit for captains and officers. Rich foreigners – Americans, Englishmen –

REGINA. Don't! –

ENGSTRAND. Cloths on the tables – clean linen on the beds... You think yourself the daughter of the house, Regina, but you've the mind of a slut. God's truth I want to do something right for once – something decent –

REGINA. What's my part in this?

ENGSTRAND. You'll run it. Or just lend a hand – whatever you liked. You can pass yourself off as a lady – well – working up here – it rubs off doesn't it? *(pause)* I'm sorry I called you a slut. You provoke me.

REGINA. Does it rub off? Could I be a lady?

ENGSTRAND. There'll have to be women. You'd be mistress – running it.

Women cheer a place up – it's what men expect –

back from a long sea voyage – music – dancing *(coming nearer)* you have to have women...

Don't turn me down, Regina – you'd be a fool to yourself.

Generous men, well-paid men.

What sort of a future would you have with Mrs Alving?

The education she's given you – the money she's laid out – you'd be wasted out here. You'd wither into a dry old spinster teaching snotty kids in the orphanage. Is that what you want?

Work your fingers to the bone for snobs like the Alvings? Eh?

You belong with your own kind.

REGINA. My own kind...

No, Father – if things go my way – and they might – they just might...

ENGSTRAND. Eh? What things?

REGINA. None of your business. How much?

ENGSTRAND. What?

REGINA. How much have you saved?

ENGSTRAND. Seven or eight hundred

REGINA. Pah! *(amused)*

ENGSTRAND. Its a start.

REGINA. You've never given me a penny.

ENGSTRAND. You've not gone short.

REGINA. You could have sent me something now and then – rich man like you, Father – spending money, jewels, dresses.

ENGSTRAND. You come with me. There'll be dresses.

REGINA. I'll bet there will!

ENGSTRAND. I've got my eye on a place in Little Harbour Street.

They're not asking much – small down payment – nice house...

Nine or ten bedrooms.

REGINA. I want nothing to do with your money, or your house, or your bedrooms. Come on – out.

ENGSTRAND. Think it over – that's all I'm asking.

I believe you'd take to it – that sort of work...

Not that you'd stay long – not if you know what's what.

You've your mother's looks. You've got her...

Some rich captain – first officer –

REGINA. Marry me off to a sailor boy, would you?

ENGSTRAND. Oh you needn't go as far as the altar, Regina –
they pay better for the other thing. Did your mother
never tell you?

REGINA. Don't you dare! –

ENGSTRAND. That Englishman she took up with – with his
great big yacht?
Oho, your mother couldn't get enough of that great
big yacht –

REGINA. You're not fit to speak my mother's name!

ENGSTRAND. Two hundred dollars she screwed out of
him – oh yes, Regina –
Two hundred dollars! –

REGINA. Liar! Liar!

ENGSTRAND. What a body she had – what looks – but yours
is –

REGINA. Get your hands off me!

ENGSTRAND. *(laughing)* Hit a poor old cripple would you –
That's enough! Just…think it over. That's all I ask.

REGINA. Go – please, please! You'll wake Osvald.

ENGSTRAND. Oh Osvald I see. Osvald is it? Osvald! Wake
up – you lazy bugger – the day's nearly over!

REGINA. Please! Father! Just leave me alone. Let him…

ENGSTRAND. Aha! I'm right then? Have you been giving
the lad his oats –

REGINA. Oh God – it's Pastor Manders!

ENGSTRAND. Jesus God, I'm not ready for him yet –

REGINA. Out the back way – quickly!

ENGSTRAND. Talk to the pastor, Regina – he'll speak up for
me.
He'll tell you a daughter's place is with her father.
And I am your father. It says so in the Parish Register.

*(REGINA shoves him out, puts herself in order, makes
herself busy.* PASTOR MANDERS *wearing an overcoat,
carrying an umbrella and a briefcase comes in out of
the rain)*

MANDERS. Good morning, Miss Engstrand.

REGINA. Good morning, Pastor. Was the steamer early?

MANDERS. *(coming into the room)* It's absolutely pouring down.

REGINA. Nice weather for ducks.

MANDERS. Hmm? What ducks?

REGINA. Good for the farmers too.

MANDERS. I'm sorry? Oh yes, I see. We city dwellers often forget. Ha! God's good rain –

REGINA. Your coat's soaked through. Give me the umbrella too – I'll… Best to leave it open –

(She takes his wet things out into the hall. He looks around. Then puts his hat and briefcase on a chair)

MANDERS. It's good to be indoors again.

REGINA. Though it's unlucky they say… To…

MANDERS. All well out here?

REGINA. Very well thank you, Pastor.

MANDERS. You must all be very busy. Hmm? Tomorrow is the great day.

REGINA. We're all so looking forward –

MANDERS. Where's… *(he is going to say "Helen")* Is Mrs Alving…?

REGINA. She's upstairs – gone to look in on the Master.

MANDERS. The…? Oh yes, I see – young Osvald.

REGINA. He arrived a day early. We weren't expecting him till this evening.

MANDERS. Ah. I trust he's in good health?

REGINA. He's exhausted. He came all the way from Paris without stopping. I mean he didn't break his journey anywhere. It's a long way isn't it –

MANDERS. I suppose it must be.

REGINA. He's still asleep. We've been tiptoeing around all morning.

MANDERS. Then we must be very quiet.

REGINA. Won't you sit down, Pastor?

MANDERS. Do you know, you were not much more than a
child when I last saw you. And now...

REGINA. I've filled out haven't I? Blossomed?

MANDERS. Well yes, so you have. Very... Very becoming.

REGINA. I'll fetch Mrs Alving –

MANDERS. No, not yet. First tell me about your father. Has
Engstrand been behaving himself out here?

REGINA. Well I've not really –

MANDERS. He came over to town a few weeks ago. Paid me
a visit.

REGINA. Did he?

MANDERS. It's good of you to keep a watchful eye on him.
He says you see him every day.

REGINA. Does he?

MANDERS. He's a weak man, Regina. Weak. Be firm with
him.

REGINA. I've always done my best for him –

MANDERS. He needs someone he can depend upon –
a guiding hand.

Left to himself he will continue to offend. He's quite
open about it.

He knows how low he's sunk. A soul in turmoil. In
grave danger – true. But he admits his weakness,
understands the temptation...

Now that should give us grounds for hope – hope of
his reclamation.

REGINA. I'm needed here – especially now we have the
orphanage to run.

I shouldn't want to leave Mrs Alving, Pastor. She's like
a mother to me.

MANDERS. Like a mother, yes. But you are Engstrand's
daughter.

Does it mean nothing to you? The ties of blood? A
child's duty?

We both know how sly he can be – Oh, he believes he
can pull the wool over my eyes whenever he wants to.
Ha! He can't.

He would ask you to make sacrifices.

And you will ask me if he deserves them. Rightly so.

Naturally we must discuss the matter with Mrs Alving.

REGINA. But, Pastor, isn't it wrong for a girl my age to keep house for an unmarried man?

MANDERS. An unmarried man? We're discussing your father –

REGINA. And he's such a... If it were for a gentleman – in a respectable household –

MANDERS. Regina –

REGINA. I don't believe I could be a daughter to him – I don't believe he thinks of me in that way –

MANDERS. What are you saying? –

REGINA. And yet... It's what I long for. I've always imagined that somewhere there's a good man who would be a proper father to me...

And I'd like to live in town again – we never see anybody out here. The loneliness gets me down sometimes.

You must know yourself what it's like to have nobody – I'm sure you know what it's like. Can't you advise me, Pastor?

I'd work hard for the right man. Do you know of anybody?

MANDERS. This won't do, Regina –

REGINA. If you hear of a good man –

MANDERS. That's enough. I'll not discuss the matter further. *(standing up)*

Think about what I've said. Will you do that?

Now perhaps you'd be good enough to fetch Mrs Alving?

REGINA. Yes, sir.

(She goes. MANDERS walks up and down. Looks into the garden. Goes over to the table. Picks up a book. Frowns. Picks up more. He registers disapproval. MRS ALVING comes in followed by REGINA who immediately goes out by the other door)

MRS ALVING. Pastor Manders. Welcome to Rosenvold. It's good to see you.

MANDERS. Well, here I am!

MRS ALVING. Was the steamer early?

MANDERS. I don't know, was it? I was lucky to catch it at all – committee meetings right up until the last moment. I take on too much.
Oh, I'm sorry – am I before my time?

MRS ALVING. It's good you're early.
We can settle the orphanage business before lunch.
Then we can talk – we have much to say to each other.
Has somebody brought your luggage in?

MANDERS. No luggage. I thought it best... I'm staying in the village.

MRS ALVING. *(suppressing a smile)* You must know you're always welcome to stay with me.

MANDERS. Yes. Thank you. But I shall...er..

MRS ALVING. As you wish. I suppose you think there'd be gossip –

MANDERS. Gossip? Certainly not! It's not that –

MRS ALVING. You're too ridiculous! Old folk like us –

MANDERS. Old folk like us?
Well what can have brought on these high spirits – the celebration isn't until tomorrow. Oh no – of course! Osvald's home – for his father's memorial. That's why you're so –

MRS ALVING. Isn't it wonderful? He's going to stay the whole winter.

MANDERS. He's a dutiful son then – to forego the attractions of Rome and Paris for a wet winter in the fjords.

MRS ALVING. For a winter with his mother. He's a good boy.

MANDERS. I'm very glad to hear it. I worry for young men who dabble in the Arts. So often it tends to coarsen them – hurries in a loss of innocence. Makes harsh their natural affections.

MRS ALVING. No danger of that with Osvald. I'm curious to see how you two will get on together – how long has it been?

MANDERS. Oh –

MRS ALVING. You were not always on the best of terms, I remember.

He should be down soon. Regina has taken him up a cup of chocolate.

MANDERS. Has she. *(it's slight disaproval, not a question)* Then… shall we make a start on these documents?

MRS ALVING. Yes. Let's get it over and done with.

MANDERS. Er… Very well. I've brought the – er –

(He goes over to the table and begins to take the papers out of the briefcase. He sits opposite MRS ALVING and begins to move the books so that he can spread out the papers)

I think we'd better look over the deeds first. *(breaks off)* May I ask you something? What are these books doing here?

MRS ALVING. I put them there. I'm reading them.

MANDERS. You are reading them? I assumed it was Osvald…

MRS ALVING. You disapprove?

MANDERS. Are you better for them in any way? Do they increase your happiness.

MRS ALVING. My happiness? Well they give me a certain confidence.

MANDERS. Confidence?

MRS ALVING. Is this really so important? – sometimes they explain – no not explain – they confirm – support things I've been trying to work out for myself.

I haven't found anything startling or indeed very new in them – most people would find very little offence in them. Not that they'd admit it.

MANDERS. You believe people would find the moral stance – or rather the lack of one – taken by these books acceptable?

MRS ALVING. Yes.

MANDERS. Decent people like ourselves or the... lower... er...?

MRS ALVING. Now you're going to be pompous. Everybody accepts that times change. There are no longer any certainties – and there is no harm in questioning accepted truths... *(amused)* What is it you actually dislike? – the ideas in these books or the fact of their publication.

MANDERS. You know I haven't read them. So – now you'll tell me I should not condemn works I know nothing of?

MRS ALVING. I shall resist the temptation.

MANDERS. These books are discussed, reviewed, quoted – I've read enough to know I've nothing to learn from them.

MRS ALVING. Can't you form your own opinion?

MANDERS. How can you be so naïve? There are very few occasions in life when one is not forced to rely upon the opinions of others. The world is founded on trust – how would we manage otherwise? I don't need to thrust my hand into a cess pit to tell you it would come out stinking.

MRS ALVING. I don't know... You might be right.

MANDERS. I'm not a fool, Helen. I can understand the fascination these works hold for some people. No doubt you have persuaded yourself that you need to keep abreast of the times – follow intellectual trends... No in your case the reason is probably simpler: you wish to grow closer to your son – converse with him. Am I not right? You fear that after the philosophical cut and thrust of Rome and Paris poor Osvald might find home and mother a little dull.

MRS ALVING. You were never afraid to speak your mind.

MANDERS. I was never afraid to confront the truth. Oh, I suppose that while this is certainly trash it's not dangerous trash. You have a brain. You'll come to no harm... but keep them to yourself. Hide them away. You shouldn't leave books lying where anybody might find them – servants, stable boys –

MRS ALVING. The lower orders.

MANDERS. I was thinking of Regina.

MRS ALVING. Yes. I shall be more careful

MANDERS. You're not obliged to account to me for what you do secretly within your own four walls – but think of the orphanage – of the children in it's care. You hold a position in society – in the public eye. At least observe the forms and decencies.

MRS ALVING. It was because I was thinking about the orphanage...

MANDERS. Go on.

MRS ALVING. No. It doesn't matter.

MANDERS. Discretion. It's not that difficult. Here – these are the deeds. *(handing them to her)* I don't mind telling you that bringing these affairs to this conclusion has provided me with a good deal of the most tedious labour I have ever endured. The law! Ha! I never suspected, when I became a man of God, how much of the Scribe and the Pharisee I would need to find within myself. Ha! This is the conveyance *(reads)* 'of the plot registered as Solvik, being part of the Rosenvold estate...mmm...mmm... together with the buildings erected thereon... the school, the staff accommodation...mmm... The chapel...' Do you want to look it over? These refer to the endowment... authorisation etcetera... rules of the Institution...

MRS ALVING. I don't need to read it through. If you say it's in order. 'The Captain Alving Children's Home' –

MANDERS. 'Memorial' – let me see. It should say 'The Captain Alving Memorial Children's Home.'

MRS ALVING. It does.

MANDERS. Is 'Captain' acceptable?

MRS ALVING. Yes...

MANDERS. It seemed somehow brisker than 'King's
Councillor Alving' – a good deal less pretentious.

MRS ALVING. Whatever you think best –

MANDERS. Keep these safe. They're the accounts of the
capital in the savings bank. The interest on these
investments will provide for the day-to-day running of
the orphanage. And these we can use to balance, after
the annual review and governors' meeting –

MRS ALVING. No. You keep them. Is that too much of an
imposition?

MANDERS. Not at all. I can oversee the accounts if you wish
it. The interest we're getting at the moment is not
particularly attractive. When we've had more time to
consider I'm sure the income can be increased. But it
will do for now.

MRS ALVING. Whatever you decide. Is that all?

MANDERS. Four percent. Hm… four percent… I should
be able to do better than that. We'll have to see. No,
there's one more thing.

MRS ALVING. What's that?

MANDERS. Insurance. Do you want the buildings insured?

MRS ALVING. Of course they must be insured! What a
question!

MANDERS. Yes. I suppose so.

MRS ALVING. Everything I have is insured – the house,
contents – farm buildings, crops, stock – I thought you
would have done that already?

MANDERS. No. On your estate, yes naturally. I do the same.
Yes… It's just… The orphanage is to be consecrated
to a higher purpose – an offering to God if you like.
And – this may seem the worst kind of superstition to
you – It's just that it feels like tempting fate to want to
insure a building in which God himself has such an
interest.

MRS ALVING. Insure the buildings. If God disapproves I'll
take the blame.

MANDERS. But, you know... I'm thinking of how it might look to the leaders of our community. Might they not say that neither you nor I showed a proper confidence in Divine Providence? Am I not their Pastor? –

MRS ALVING. Then do as you please! What do you want me to say? If you feel strongly that –

MANDERS. But on the other hand these same people have great hopes of the orphanage. They expect it will relieve a great part of the burden of our local taxes. If disaster struck and we could not make good the damage... After all, I am your adviser. I would be blamed –

MRS ALVING. Then clearly we must be fully insured.

MANDERS. Yes... And I must prepare myself to face the attacks that will certainly be made upon me in those newspapers and periodicals which –

MRS ALVING. I really don't want to think about it any more. You decide what is best for the orphanage and for the community. I leave it entirely to you.

MANDERS. But if I did leave it uninsured and...disaster struck... Could you afford to rebuild?

MRS ALVING. Definitely not. Nor would I want to.

MANDERS. We're taking a great deal upon ourselves.

MRS ALVING. I should be sorry to think that the help and advice you have given so freely should be used to undermine your standing in the community.

MANDERS. Or in the Church. I'm in a very difficult and painful position.

MRS ALVING. I think we can safely assume that whatever you decide God will keep His watchful eye on the orphanage. (smiles)

MANDERS. It's not a matter for levity. Not for me, anyway... There are one or two documents – no three in fact – on which I shall need a signature. Yes. Here. Here. And here. (she signs the three documents)

MRS ALVING. Is that it?

MANDERS. Yes, yes. I'll just… I was talking to Regina before you came down… about her father.

MRS ALVING. Good. I hope you're going to speak to him while you're here.

MANDERS. Poor man! There are so many temptations for him. There! That's it. *(stuffs papers in his briefcase)* What were you saying?

MRS ALVING. About Engstrand.

MANDERS. Poor soul. He tries so hard. He's so desperate to change his ways.

MRS ALVING. Do you think so? Who told you that?

MANDERS. He told me so himself. I'm very pleased with the work he's been doing at the orphanage. He's a master of his craft.

MRS ALVING. He's certainly crafty.

MANDERS. If only he could stay sober! He claims that his foot gives him a lot of pain – and the pain drives him to drink. Of course it's nonsense –

MRS ALVING. Yes it is –

MANDERS. But he can be sincere you know. The last time he was in town he came and thanked me for finding him work here. Quite touching really… And he tells me it makes a great difference to him to be near his daughter.

MRS ALVING. Nonsense! Regina's hardly spoken to him all the time he's been here.

MANDERS. No, you're wrong about that. She goes to see him every day – he told me so. They pray together. I was saying to Regina, the thing about Jakob Engstrand is that he's prepared to confess his failings. If a man is to be a soul at peace, the first step towards that peace must be his admitting to himself that he has a struggle ahead of him. Engstrand is ready and willing – eager almost – to parade his weaknesses in front of the whole community. Ha! He can be quite amusing. What he needs is support. He should have someone –

MRS ALVING. No.

MANDERS. I'm sorry?

MRS ALVING. I see where this is leading.

MANDERS. If it should become necessary –

MRS ALVING. No –

MANDERS. For Regina –

MRS ALVING. I won't allow it –

MANDERS. She's his daughter. Who else can look after him?

MRS ALVING. Not Regina.

MANDERS. It's wrong of you to try to prevent it.

MRS ALVING. I shall prevent it. Regina is needed at the orphanage.

MANDERS. She's needed by her father. His salvation could depend upon it.

MRS ALVING. You know perfectly well what sort of a father he has been. He's a drunk – a brute – and I very much suspect –

MANDERS. In the past he may –

MRS ALVING. She's never going back to him. Not with my blessing.

MANDERS. Don't be so agitated about it –

MRS ALVING. I have my reasons –

MANDERS. You're misjudging Engstrand. Cruelly... I don't know what to think –

MRS ALVING. Think what you like. I've taken Regina into my house and here she stays. Please don't raise this matter again – my mind is made up. (enter OSVALD) Osvald!

OSVALD. I'm sorry. I thought you'd be in the study. (He has an unlit pipe in his mouth. Coming in) Good morning, Pastor.

MANDERS. I'm amazed –

MRS ALVING. Well, what do you think of him?

MANDERS. Can this be little Osvald?

OSVALD. Yes. The return of the prodigal son –

MANDERS. Osvald –

OSVALD. Well 'the son.' In fairness to myself I'd better drop
the 'prodigal' –

MANDERS. My dear boy, how good to see you! How are you!

MRS ALVING. Look at him and confess you were wrong. You
were so determined he should not become an artist –

MANDERS. I gave my advice firmly –

MRS ALVING. Like a bully. *(teasing)*

MANDERS. – because I was asked for it. I have never
claimed to be infallible. Anyway, it was a long time ago.
Welcome home, I'm delighted to see you, Osvald. I
may still call you Osvald? I suppose I was a little hard
on the poor artists – one reads such things – Paris –
it can't all be loose morals, absinthe drinkers, and
starving in garrets. At any rate, you don't look as if
that's been your life.

OSVALD. I managed to keep myself out of most of the
garrets.

MRS ALVING. A pure heart in a pure body.

(She tries to hold him as a mother would a small child.
He pulls away and paces around the room)

OSVALD. Don't embarrass me, Mother…

MANDERS. You've been making quite an impression. It's
good to see the name Alving up there with all those
Frenchmen and Italians. Even our local papers have
reviewed your exhibitions – very favourably –

OSVALD. Not recently though –

MANDERS. I can't remember the last –

OSVALD. *(he is not looking at* MANDERS*)* It was over a year
ago. An exhibition of Italian landscapes. I've not been
painting much this summer.

MRS ALVING. He's having a well-earned rest.

MANDERS. I'm sure, I'm sure. So how have you been
spending your time? Planning a masterpiece? A
revolution in style? Are you going to astound us all –

OSVALD. Well you'll just have to wait and see, won't you?

MRS ALVING. Osvald –

OSVALD. When are we eating?

MRS ALVING. In about half an hour – sooner perhaps.

MANDERS. Nothing wrong with a young man's appetite.

MRS ALVING. I –

MANDERS. The pipe!

OSVALD. Yes – it was Father's. I found it in his room –

MANDERS. Of course! That's what it was –

MRS ALVING. What?

MANDERS. The pipe. When I saw Osvald standing in the doorway, it could almost have been his father. The pipe was the finishing touch.

OSVALD. Really? Do you think I'm so like him?

MRS ALVING. He's not a bit like Alving. You're like me – everybody says so.

MANDERS. Allow me to disagree. Look at the corner of his mouth – the way the pipe pulls it down – exactly how I remember Alving.

MRS ALVING. Nonsense. Don't light it in here, Osvald – not in here.

OSVALD. I wasn't going to. I've not smoked it since I was a child.

MANDERS. *(laughs)* What can you mean!

OSVALD. I'll never forget it – it was – I would have been about five or six. I went up to Father's room. He was in one of his jolly moods – very jolly –

MRS ALVING. You must have dreamed it.

OSVALD. No – I remember it quite clearly. Father lifted me up onto his knee and made me smoke his pipe. This pipe. 'Smoke it, my boy,' he said, 'go on, smoke away, smoke!' And, being a trusting sort of child, I gulped at it as hard as I could. I turned green – the sweat stood out on my forehead. And all the time he was roaring with laughter –

MANDERS. That doesn't sound like Alving.

MRS ALVING. It's Osvald's imagination –

OSVALD. No, Mother – you were there. You came in, picked me up, and carried me into the nursery. Then I was sick – very sick. I remember you crying. Strange thing for my father to do. He was usually so – I don't know – reserved? Wasn't he?

MANDERS. He lived life to the full, especially when he was a young man.

OSVALD. And he died so young.

MANDERS. Yes – but in the short time God allotted to him he achieved much that was good and useful. And he left you his good name. I'm sure you'll be worthy of it.

OSVALD. I've always tried to be.

MANDERS. Tomorrow we shall honour his memory. You show yourself a dutiful son – to interrupt your work and come home for the ceremonies.

OSVALD. Least I could do. For one's father. Besides, I told you, I've not been painting much.

MRS ALVING. I shall have him all to myself for weeks and weeks and months –

MANDERS. I hear you're planning to stay with us through the winter?

OSVALD. Perhaps. I don't make plans. I just need to be home for a while.

MRS ALVING. I wish he'd stay with me forever!

MANDERS. You were so very young when you went out into the world.

OSVALD. I was. Too young, really.

MRS ALVING. You were a lively healthy child – you wouldn't have thanked me for keeping you tied to my apron strings – no brother or sister – no companions of your own age –

MANDERS. I thought it a curious decision on your part, Helen – though having no wife nor children of my own, how could I know?

My instincts would be... Well, I think I'd want to watch my children growing up around me.

OSVALD. Well said! Good for you, Pastor. I'm with you there.

MANDERS. You've produced an odd creature, my dear. He's what – twenty five or six – old enough to start his own family – but he can have no conception of what a home should be. He's never experienced family life.

OSVALD. You're wrong.

MANDERS. Oh? I'm sorry. I imagined student life – young artists...

OSVALD. Go on?

MANDERS. Well one doesn't think of that sort of existence as having much to do with family life. Especially the – er – younger...

OSVALD. Ah!

MANDERS. Getting married, setting up home, having children. That comes later, doesn't it. When one can afford it. And as you spent your own childhood away –

OSVALD. Many of my friends had homes – pleasant comfortable homes. Not all of them could afford to be married.

MANDERS. I think we're both trying to say the same thing. I don't mean young men sharing lodgings, I was talking about a home – a family home – where a good Christian man lives with his wife and children.

OSVALD. Or the mother of his children.

MANDERS. Lives with the mother of his children? Unmarried?

OSVALD. Yes. Would you rather he abandoned her?

MANDERS. What type of man would place a young girl in that situation?
What type of girl would allow herself to be used like that?

OSVALD. Type? Types? What else can they do? Marriage – setting up home as you say – is way beyond the reach of

the young people I knew in Paris. Have you considered
the cost? Years of saving and scraping –

MANDERS. Are they animals? The young should exercise
self-restraint – strengthen the spiritual side of love –
and not bring children into the world until they can
afford to give them the sort of home every child has
the right to expect – demand – of a responsible, loving
parent.

OSVALD. We must live in the real world, Pastor. Your
argument wouldn't carry much weight with the warm –
blooded youth of France and Italy.

MRS ALVING. I imagine it wouldn't.

MANDERS. You think not? This from the woman who is
about to found an orphanage. 'Do as I do. Follow me,
follow me,' said the lamb at the slaughter-house door.
I was right to fear for your son, Mrs Alving. I find he's
been living in darkness – among people for whom
life holds very few mysteries, and for whom decency,
responsibility, and love are subjects for mockery.

OSVALD. Oh come! How could you know? If you'd lived
among them – as I have… What are you afraid of?
What do you imagine goes on? Let me tell you. I've
never witnessed any indecent act – never listened to a
single objectionable or immoral conversation –

MANDERS. Really? What paragons they all sound – what
sentimental pictures you paint – 'Sunday with the
Family' –

OSVALD. Do you want to know where I have come across
immorality? Real immorality? –

MANDERS. I'm sure you're going to tell me –

OSVALD. In upright, decent, family men – in businessman
exploring Paris – in the model husband and father –
the good Christian knows where to look – all the
streets to loiter in – all the places to go.

MANDERS. Aha – the businessman abroad! What a very
uncomplicated type he must be – so predictable in his
vices –

OSVALD. They go home to their families and rant and rave about the immorality gripping the great cities of Europe – blah, blah, blah! They know all about immorality. They created it.

MRS ALVING. You know he's right.

MANDERS. He's a child! Still a child, I find. He sees the world with a child's eyes. Sin is subtle – If goodness and vice were as recognisable as Osvald seems to think they are, we clergymen should have a very easy time of it. The roots of evil reach far deeper than he could understand.

OSVALD. My friends are hardworking, honest, and deep-thinking people. Why do you shut your mind to what I'm saying? I speak only the truth whether you like it or not. Perhaps you're the sort who prefers to believe the scandal?

MRS ALVING. My dear, the Pastor is a guest in your house. Calm down, calm down!

OSVALD. I'm sorry. I'm so tired you see – and I need some fresh air... Will this rain ever stop? You must forgive me, Pastor. I know you can't accept my views, but I can't let that stop me expressing them. *(exit)*

MRS ALVING. Poor thing!

MANDERS. Self-righteous young prig! He was right to call himself the Prodigal Son. What arrogance! *(***MRS ALVING** *watches him pace up and down but says nothing)* Haven't you anything to say for yourself? Helen?

MRS ALVING. I agree with him.

MANDERS. *(angry)* For yourself! I said, for yourself!

MRS ALVING. Myself! When have I ever been allowed a view of my own? A lonely woman stuck out here to run a country estate – 'Get on with it, Helen! Get on with it!' I do have views. I have formed opinions. I've never had the courage or the opportunity to share them – or anybody to share them with for the last ten years.

MANDERS. That's enough. Let me speak to you as your priest – not your adviser, nor your friend. Your priest.

You will remember the last occasion when I was forced
to do so.

MRS ALVING. How could I forget?

MANDERS. Tomorrow is the tenth anniversary of your
husband's death. There is to be a celebration of his
life. We shall open the orphanage and I shall speak
about the Alvings in front of the whole town. First I
must speak to you alone.

MRS ALVING. Then please do, Pastor Manders.

MANDERS. Less than a year after you made your solemn vows
before God's holy altar you abandoned your home,
your husband, and walked out of your marriage. In
spite of all Alving's prayers and entreaties you refused
to go back to him.

MRS ALVING. I was utterly wretched in that first year.

MANDERS. Why were you wretched? Why? Did you imagine
that happiness in marriage would descend from
Heaven the moment you mumbled your vows? Instead
of working and praying for the gift of happiness, you
rebelled – ran away from your duties – abandoned the
husband you had sworn to support and cherish. You
were spineless – gutless.

MRS ALVING. If I'd known the kind of man Alving was
before I made those vows...
But you knew what he was – you knew!

MANDERS. How can one man truly know another? Does a
priest condemn the souls in his care on the evidence
of malicious gossip? I despise weakness in the young –
where it is most usually tolerated. Had I known
anything against Alving I should not have spared him.
That's not at issue. We're talking of your own failing.
You should have faced the difficulties in your marriage
and overcome them. That was your duty. Marriage is
a trial of our faith, it lays open every weakness in our
souls. If it's true that Alving, as a young man, had been
weak, then your vows required you to reform and save
him. You had sworn to accept with patience the good
and the bad. With patience and humility. Instead you

ran away, risking the good name of your family – and endangering other people's reputations –

MRS ALVING. 'Other people's reputations'? You mean yours.

MANDERS. I do! It was reckless and cruel of you to come to me.

MRS ALVING. What? To go to our priest? Our great friend?

MANDERS. You abused a double trust. I thank God I was able to crush your rebellious spirit and show you the true way back to faith.

MRS ALVING. Oh you certainly did that!

MANDERS. It was God's doing. I was merely his instrument. Without His grace I should have been powerless to help you. And I was right to do so wasn't I? The moment you showed a little spirit Alving began to live only for your happiness. He became the town's greatest benefactor. I showed you the part you had to play, and – to your credit – you played it well.

MRS ALVING. It was not a role I was fitted for.

MANDERS. But having failed once as a wife you have also failed – and it's a deeper failure – as a mother.

MRS ALVING. Oh…

MANDERS. All your life you've been selfish. Your energies have been dissipated in testing, questioning what you know by instinct and advice to be good and proper. You won't accept truth for its own sake and you've always tried to evade anything that is difficult or challenging. After a few months you're bored with your marriage so you decide you'll walk away from it! After a few years you're bored with being a mother so poor Osvald must be packed off to boarding school!

MRS ALVING. It's true. I did that –

MANDERS. Which is why you hardly know him now.

MRS ALVING. You're wrong –

MANDERS. (*furious*) I am not wrong! Can you say you know how he thinks – even what he thinks of you? He's a stranger here – and look what he's turned into. Not an original thought in his head, and an inability to reason morally and logically. A self-satisfied little prig! He is merely a type. You treated your husband very shabbily didn't you? That why you wish to found this orphanage – this memorial – it's pure guilt isn't it? Conscience money.

MRS ALVING. Perhaps.

MANDERS. And how will you pay for the guilt you will come to feel over Osvald? Another orphanage? It is my duty to tell you that, as a mother, you're an utter failure.

MRS ALVING. *(she seems stunned – broken)* Am I? *(collects herself)* Will you now listen to what I have to say –

MANDERS. Yes – yes! *(gently)* If you wish to discuss a way forward.

MRS ALVING. I'd like a way forward. Though it may be complicated by a few simple truths. Truths it may be difficult to step over.

MANDERS. Helen, believe me – I wish only to help you.

MRS ALVING. You never really knew Alving. After you forced me to go back to him you never set foot in our house again.

MANDERS. You moved out here. It's a day's journey.

MRS ALVING. A day's journey? You called yourself our friend! In the ten years we lived out here you never found a day to visit us?

MANDERS. *(change of manner)* If that is meant to wound me then I can only beg you to consider –

MRS ALVING. That you're a priest? Yes I was selfish – a disloyal wife. Priests must stay above suspicion. Keep away from loose women.

MANDERS. We both know my reasons.

MRS ALVING. Do we? Do I? But the point – The judgment you have so eloquently – and severely – passed on me, can only be based on supposition. What did you say a moment ago? 'Should a priest condemn the souls in his care on the evidence of gossip?' You never came here to find out the truth. So now I shall tell it.

MANDERS. Go on.

MRS ALVING. My husband never changed his ways. He was a drinker – and a lecher before I met him and he remained so until the day he died.

MANDERS. I don't believe you!

MRS ALVING. Nineteen years of married life! You were talking about self-restraint. The only restraint Alving ever knew was the lack of opportunity. It was easier to leash him in out here. Out of town.

MANDERS. Are you saying that you hold a few youthful indiscretions –

MRS ALVING. Indiscretions? He was completely dissolute – pathogenically he...

MANDERS. What!

MRS ALVING. Our doctor told me –

MANDERS. Do you understand what you're saying? Helen, if this is true!

MRS ALVING. Look at me! It is the truth.

MANDERS. Dear God! Dear God! *(pause)* What have I done to you? Oh, Helen... Never, never think that I knew. Had I suspected I would certainly have... But how could it be possible? In such a community, among my own people – Am I blind?... Who else knew? In whom did you confide?

MRS ALVING. Nobody. All my energies went into keeping it secret – my dark secret. When Osvald was born – for a little while after – I thought I was winning. Then it became worse, and I had to work twice as hard. What would the child have suffered if people had known the sort of corrupt thing his father had become? Think of the child! I always put the child first. Do you not see? My child – my child!

MANDERS. I do see. At last I do see.

MRS ALVING. Some things worked in my favour. You know how plausible Alving was – he fooled you – he could charm the birds from the trees – nobody

wanted to think ill of him. He was discreet – kept his
debaucheries away from the happy home – from his
child's home. At first.

MANDERS. Is there more?

MRS ALVING. Much, much more.

MANDERS. He brought...? Into this house?

MRS ALVING. The family home – yes. I first realised what
was going on – they were in there. The maid was doing
something or other – watering the plants. Then I
heard my husband. *(a short laugh)* I can still hear him.
Them. And not without a cold chill, here. The maid
said 'Not here, Sir. Leave me alone, Sir. Let me go.'

MANDERS. No – *(gets up and walks around)*

MRS ALVING. It wasn't a youthful indiscretion. Don't shake
your head, he took her into my bed. He gave her a
child –

MANDERS. In this house –

MRS ALVING. If these walls could bear witness to what I've
suffered 'in this house' – To keep him home I've had
to sit drinking with him – clinking glasses, listening to
his filth – the whining, the self-pity – I've had to fight
with him – physically fight with him – to force him to
stay –

MANDERS. Such things don't happen.

MRS ALVING. Oh, they happen.

MANDERS. Where could you have found strength? How
could you have born it?

MRS ALVING. I found the strength. I bore it – for my
little boy. The affair with my own maid was the final
humiliation. I put an end to it. To everything. I took
control of the house, the estate – absolute control and
he could do nothing. I had a power over him you see –
his standing in the community, his good name, his
bastard... You see why I had to send Osvald away? Why
I failed as a mother?

MANDERS. Don't, Helen –

MRS ALVING. Osvald was a child but... he noticed things – you know what children are like at that age... No, you don't know. The atmosphere in this house would have poisoned him – sucked the life from him. As long as his father was alive I had to keep him away. Can you understand what that cost me? His mother?

MANDERS. I need time to think.

MRS ALVING. All the improvements to the estate – that was my work – that's what kept me sane. Naturally Alving took all the credit. The man of the house – the King's Councillor. On days when he managed to get out of bed he lay on that sofa reading the Court Circular. It was all my work.

MANDERS. And this is the man to whom you are raising a memorial.

MRS ALVING. Yes. A monument to my bad conscience.

MANDERS. *Yours!*

MRS ALVING. I want something worthy and decent to blot out any memories of what he was really like. The orphanage will hide the truth. Our good name will be preserved – Osvald's good name. I've always feared that the truth would get out one day.

MANDERS. Pray God it never does! The truth – don't speak of it!

MRS ALVING. Shall I tell you what I've done? I calculated the value of Alving's fortune at the time I married him – the capital that made our match so attractive to my parents. That amount I've put into the orphanage. I've repaid every tainted penny. Everything Osvald inherits will come from me – from my hard work over all those years. I've obliterated his father's –

MANDERS. Shh! *(he indicates that* OSVALD *is coming into the room)*

MRS ALVING. Osvald! Aren't you soaking.

OSVALD. I don't think I'll ever be warm and dry. Isn't it time to eat yet?

REGINA. *(coming in)*

There's a parcel for you, Madam.

MRS ALVING. Thank you. *(glancing at* **MANDERS**) It will be the music for the choirs tomorrow.

MANDERS. Hm…

REGINA. And dinner is served.

MRS ALVING. We'll be in in a minute – I just want to open this. *(She does so)*

REGINA. Red wine or white wine, Mr Alving?

OSVALD. Both, I think.

REGINA. Mais oui, Bien. *(exit into dining room)*

OSVALD. *(following her, amused)* Do you want me to uncork it? *(the door to the dining room is half open)*

MRS ALVING. Yes, It's the scores for the choir.

MANDERS. How am I going to get through tomorrow? I have to make that speech.

MRS ALVING. You'll manage.

MANDERS. I shall have to. There must be no hint of scandal.

MRS ALVING. And then it will be over. An exorcism – my house free of its demons. No memories here – no ghosts – just me. And Osvald.

(From the dining room comes the noise of a chair falling and **REGINA**'s *subdued voice)*

REGINA. Mr Alving! Let me go. Don't *(laughs)* I'll spill it…

MRS ALVING. *(chilled)* Oh.

*(***OSVALD** *can be heard humming and coughing. a bottle is opened)*

MANDERS. What's the matter? Helen – what's wrong?

MRS ALVING. Ghosts. The two of them. Back in the house.

MANDERS. What? You mean Regina…? Regina is Alving's… Alving's…?

MRS ALVING. Yes. Don't say a word. Shall we go in? *(she takes his arm and they go into the dining room)*

END OF ACT ONE

ACT TWO

(MRS ALVING and PASTOR MANDERS come out of the dining room)

MRS ALVING. *(calling into the dining room)* Aren't you going to join us, Osvald?

OSVALD. I don't think so. I might go out for a walk.

MRS ALVING. I should. I think it's clearing up. *(she calls into the dining room)* Regina!

REGINA. *(off)* I'm coming.

MRS ALVING. Would you go down to the wash-house? They'll need some help with the decorations. *(REGINA is slow to leave the dining room)* Come on! Come on! *(to herself)*

REGINA. I was just going, Mrs Alving. *(she makes sure that REGINA has gone and shuts the door)*

MANDERS. Can he hear us?

MRS ALVING. No.

MANDERS. I could hardly eat a thing.

MRS ALVING. What are we to do?

MANDERS. I don't know – can't think. I'm completely out of my depth. Do you suspect there's something between them?

MRS ALVING. There hasn't been time. But she must leave this house.

MANDERS. Yes. At once.

MRS ALVING. But I can't just… Where could I possibly send her?

MANDERS. Isn't it obvious? To her father as I suggested.

MRS ALVING. Where?

MANDERS. To her father! *(pause as he realises what he's said)* Dear God, what am I saying! Can you be absolutely sure about this?

MRS ALVING. Johanna confessed. Alving didn't deny it. There's no mistake.

MANDERS. Dear God!

MRS ALVING. The girl was packed off back to town – she was well paid and kept her mouth shut – took up with Engstrand. I believe she concocted some story about a rich Englishman with a yacht. Engstrand didn't mind – he had the money –

MANDERS. And I married them! They faced me in front of the altar and... How could Engstrand have made such a fool of me! I remember distinctly – he came, grovelling, repentant – reproached himself bitterly for making her pregnant – she was little more than a child –

MRS ALVING. Yes. He's quick to take the blame if he can work it to his advantage –

MANDERS. He made a mockery of the sacrament of marriage for – what did you give her? –

MRS ALVING. Five hundred dollars.

MANDERS. Sinks into life of vice for a miserable five hundred dollars!

MRS ALVING. And what of my life – bound to a vicious man? You knew!

MANDERS. But Dear God! –

MRS ALVING. What's the difference? Was Alving any purer when you married me to him?

MANDERS. There's all the difference in the world –

MRS ALVING. Is there? Is there? The only difference was the price.

MANDERS. No, Helen. Your eyes were open when you married Alving. Your parents were in full agreement – you were in love with him.

MRS ALVING. I must have deceived myself then. *(pause)* You knew perfectly well with whom I was in love.

MANDERS. *(with difficulty)* If I'd suspected anything of the sort I would have... stayed away from you.

MRS ALVING. You were with us almost every day. Love had no part in my marriage. I was pushed into it – bullied into it by my mother and aunts. I wasn't old enough to make up my own mind. Don't say you don't remember – 'I'd be mad to refuse him... Such a rich man – so handsome – so full of life!' I wonder what mother would say if she could see what she has done.

MANDERS. She couldn't possibly have foreseen – nobody could –

MRS ALVING. *(tapping on the window pane)* I should never have hidden the truth about Alving. The truth! I was such a coward in those days.

MANDERS. A coward?

MRS ALVING. Think what people would have said! 'Poor man! Who can blame him – with a wife who deserted him.'

MANDERS. Was there not also a measure of truth in that?

MRS ALVING. *(looks fixedly at him)* Oh yes. It was true. We should always tell the truth. I'll go in there to Osvald and say 'I'm going to tell you the truth about your father – whose memory you worship. He was a vicious lecher – a drunk –' and our maid's your half sister –

MANDERS. Stop! God forbid!

MRS ALVING. I'm a coward still.

MANDERS. It can't be cowardice – to protect your son. It's important that he continues to honour the memory of his father. Let the dead rest in peace. What good would it do to burden Osvald with these horrors?

MRS ALVING. You're my priest. What's your advice – tell me? Should Osvald have loved and honoured Alving while he was alive? No. Why should he love and honour him now he's dead. Where's your logic?

MANDERS. I know that there is something in your heart forbidding you to destroy the boy's illusion – the ideals he should cherish –

MRS ALVING. Ideals! What about the truth!

MANDERS. Every boy needs a father to look up to – he needs ideals. It seems to me that Osvald has lost most of his – but his father remains for him. All your life you have been encouraging your son to think of Alving as a model of propriety – nobility – he lives on as a hero in the boy's eyes. Isn't that a kind of truth?

MRS ALVING. To preserve that 'kind of truth' I've been lying to him for years. He thinks I sent him away!

MANDERS. He needs that illusion. That faith –

MRS ALVING. Does he? I see I'd make a rotten theologian. One thing is clear – Regina must leave this house. I won't have another life ruined.

MANDERS. No.

MRS ALVING. If I thought he were serious about the girl – or that she'd make him happy... But she's not... suitable. It would be so easy to say take her – live with her – anything you like. Let there be an end to all this deceit.

MANDERS. That's monstrous! I won't sit here and listen to you raving like this! A liaison with his own father's bastard – it's an outrage!

MRS ALVING. Worse things have happened – and been stifled, and buried –

MANDERS. I simply will not listen. I no longer understand you, Helen.

MRS ALVING. Don't you? Who made us like this, Pastor? Who but God arranged the world in this way?

MANDERS. That's enough! You're in no frame of mind to contemplate such a question. Be afraid of going down that road.

MRS ALVING. I am afraid. I'm afraid of everything. This house is full of ghosts. When I heard Osvald and Regina out there it was ghosts I was hearing – I see them everywhere! We may even be ghosts ourselves, Pastor – it's not just the things we inherit from our parents that live on in us – we're possessed by dead spirits, dead ideas, old dead beliefs. They're no longer alive but they're buried deep inside us just the same, and we can't free ourselves of them. When I pick up a newspaper ghosts materialise between the lines. I look out there – everywhere there are spirits – everywhere – in numbers like grains of sand. And we're all – all of us – so pathetically afraid of the light.

MANDERS. *(who is by the table picks up one of the books)* One doesn't have to look very far to see where your rebellious spirit comes from.

MRS ALVING. You're wrong – it came from you. You forced me to think for myself. And I'm grateful to you. *(he throws down the book)* When you made me go back to my husband – Led me 'back to the path of duty and obedience' – you spoke with such fervour about what was good and proper – when I knew that what you were making me return to was filthy and degrading. That's when I began to examine the stuff your religion is made of. I unpicked a single stitch and the whole fabric fell apart in my hands.

MANDERS. *(moved)* And this is what it has come to!

MRS ALVING. I'm your bitterest defeat.

MANDERS. It was myself I defeated.

MRS ALVING. And that too was a sin – a sin against us both.

MANDERS. It was a blessing! I refused you – took you back to the man you married. How can that be a sin?

MRS ALVING. It was a sin.

MANDERS. Then duty, truth, faith mean nothing.

MRS ALVING. Not anymore.

MANDERS. You were another man's wife. I never – not even in my most secret dreams – dared to think of you in any other way.

MRS ALVING. For once in your life, Manders – speak from your heart! Speak the truth!

MANDERS. Helen!

MRS ALVING. Is it so difficult to say what you felt?

MANDERS. *(he looks at her for a time)* Not for me. I remember
perfectly.

MRS ALVING. Well, well, well. *(change of mood)* Dead and
buried isn't it? That's enough of the past – we're
over and done with. You're up to your eyes in boring
committee work, and here I am fighting my evil
demons – the ones inside me. And out.

MANDERS. *(pause. He comes downstage not looking at her. Quietly
but firmly)* After all the things I've heard I can't, in all
conscience, let you keep Regina in this house.

MRS ALVING. What do you propose? Smuggle her back
to town and marry her off to one of Engstrand's
tap-room cronies?

MANDERS. A suitable marriage may be her only salvation.
She has reached an age – I'm no good at this sort of
thing, but we must protect her in some way. Her father
has behaved abominably. Dear God, there I go again!
Her father! *(there is a knock on the door)*

MRS ALVING. Come in!

ENGSTRAND. *(opens the door. He is wearing his Sunday clothes)*
I beg your pardon, Madam. (MANDERS, *angry, turns his
back on him)*

MRS ALVING. Engstrand. This is a surprise! We were just
talking about you.

ENGSTRAND. There wasn't any servants around – I did
knock – shouted out –

MRS ALVING. Well, come in. What did you wish to see me
about.

ENGSTRAND. Thank you, Madam. But it was the Pastor.
I was hoping to catch him. Before…

MANDERS. Were you?

ENGSTRAND. I was, Sir. If you'd be so kind.

MANDERS. Go on.

ENGSTRAND. It was just that… We've been paid off now
down at the orphanage – Thank you, Madam – and
now that the work's finished it seemed that as the

Pastor was here it would be right and proper – for all of us that've been working on it for so long – to finish up with a bit of a church service – in the chapel. We all think the same. So they sent me up here. I hope I'm not speaking out of turn.

MANDERS. 'A bit of a church service?'

ENGSTRAND. Wouldn't it be fitting, Sir?

MANDERS. Would it?

ENGSTRAND. I've been saying a few prayers there myself each evening. But they all thought – what with the Pastor being here...

MANDERS. You've been saying your prayers have you, Engstrand?

ENGSTRAND. I've got no gift for it, Sir. I'm a plain man, plain spoken. But as you was here the boys thought –

MANDERS. Are you speaking to me with a clear conscience, Engstrand?

ENGSTRAND. How do you mean?

MANDERS. Think carefully before you answer.

ENGSTRAND. Oh God love you, Pastor – sorry Ma'am – but I don't like to think about my conscience.

MANDERS. I am your priest – your conscience is my business and we're going to discuss it.

ENGSTRAND. It's a bad conscience, Sir. I'm a weak man.

MANDERS. Indeed you are. Tell me – think carefully because I want only the truth – tell me about your daughter.

MRS ALVING. Pastor Manders –

MANDERS. *(reassuringly)* Please leave this to me, Helen.

ENGSTRAND. What's the matter with her? Is she all right? O God, Sir –

MANDERS. Engstrand –

ENGSTRAND. You're giving me such a fright – what have I done? Is anything wrong with Regina?

MANDERS. Let's hope not. Who is Regina's father? Well? Come on man, answer me.

ENGSTRAND. *(uncertainly)* Sir... You know about that –

MANDERS. I thought I did. You're a liar, Engstrand – a shameless liar. Your late wife told Mrs Alving the whole story.

ENGSTRAND. Oh –

MANDERS. I've caught you out.

ENGSTRAND. And she gave me her Bible oath –

MANDERS. *(furious)* Her Bible oath!

ENGSTRAND. Johanna swore to me nobody knew.

MANDERS. You lied, and hid the truth from me all these years. What effect do you think that has had on your conscience? On your soul – to lie to your priest and to persist in that lie! You abused the faith I've placed in you!

ENGSTRAND. You're the only man what's ever been fair with me, Sir.

MANDERS. And this is how I am repaid. The baptismal entry I made in the Parish Register is mere fiction – a sham! You owe me the truth and you pay me out in tricks and lies. If you stay here a moment longer I shall lose my temper. You're a degenerate – lost, worthless, a fraud. Your whole life is a scandal. And I wash my hands of you. Get out of my sight! *(on the verge of tears)*

ENGSTRAND. *(sighs)* I'm sorry. You're quite right, Sir. *(tears)*

MANDERS. There's no possible excuse for you.

ENGSTRAND. There isn't, Sir. And there's none for her – but it was her what I was doing it for.

MANDERS. For her!

ENGSTRAND. My Johanna couldn't have lived with the shame, Sir – if people had known. If you had known... Try and put yourself in her position –

MANDERS. Engstrand!

ENGSTRAND. Oh, Dear God – I never meant to say that, Sir. What I mean is if you – if somebody had something that was so shaming in the eyes of the world – she couldn't have survived people knowing it, Sir. She wouldn't have gone on living, Pastor. I couldn't judge her. We shouldn't judge her so hard, Sir.

MANDERS. I'm not judging her. It's you I blame.

ENGSTRAND. But I thought it was my place to help her, Sir. Oh, she was a sinner... but the Book says we ought to give sinners a leg up doesn't it?

(MRS ALVING stifles a cynical laugh. MANDERS looks sharply at her)

MANDERS. Don't think you can wheedle your way out of this. Engstrand. I shall never again believe anything you say.

ENGSTRAND. But I gave her my word, Sir! *(tears)* My word of honour! Should a man break his word, Sir? Would you?

MANDERS. Of course not! What are you suggesting?

ENGSTRAND. When that Englishman got her pregnant –

MANDERS. Englishman? *(he looks at MRS ALVING)*

ENGSTRAND. She said an Englishman – or maybe an American – When she came back to town... I felt sorry for her. I know she'd done wrong – but who was I to cast the first stone? – I was never no angel myself. And twice before I'd asked her to marry me and she'd turned me down. Hardly surprising, the way I am – the way I look – but I truly loved her. That is the truth, Sir. And when she came to me and confessed and threw herself on my mercy, what could I say? What would you have said? I swore that nobody should know but the two of us.

MANDERS. Then you were a fool.

ENGSTRAND. It was make an honest woman of her or throw her back in the gutter and I just couldn't do that, Sir. It's not Jakob Engstrand's way. It near broke my heart.

MANDERS. No! You made a cynical bargain with her because of the money she brought you? Isn't that the truth?

ENGSTRAND. What money? She didn't have nothing when I took her in.

MANDERS. *(referring it to* MRS ALVING*)* Engstrand, I know
how much she was given.

ENGSTRAND. Oh wait a minute, now I know what you
mean. She told me the Englishman had left a few
dollars conscience money –

MANDERS. Five hundred dollars –

ENGSTRAND. I never knew – How much? – Five... but I
told her to fling it after him, back into the sea. He'd
cleared off on his yacht as soon as he knew how things
were with her. She didn't want his filthy money – wages
of sin – I'd have made her throw it in his face if he'd
still been around. *(weeps)*

MANDERS. So what did you do with it?

ENGSTRAND. Me? I never touched it. She told me she put
it towards Regina's upbringing and that she could
account for every dollar. I wasn't interested. I wanted
nothing to do with it.

MANDERS. *(confused)* Oh, I no longer know! – what to
believe.

ENGSTRAND. I've told you the *truth*, Sir. At last I've been
able to. And whatever happens to me – I must say I
feel better for getting it off my chest. It's been a great
burden to me all these years. I know I've been weak.

MANDERS. *(sighs)* Oh yes. We are all weak.

ENGSTRAND. Not you, Sir. You've always been a tower of
strength in my eyes. In my own defence, Sir – you have
to admit that I was a good husband to Johanna, and I
tried to bring Regina up as if she were my own. Like
the Book says we should. I made a good home for
them and I've never boasted and bragged about what
I've done, or expected a word of thanks from anybody.
But it was never off my conscience. That's why I've
failed so often – given in to the drink – not that I've
been troubled that way recently – That's why I'm so
often on your doorstep, Sir.

(pause)

MANDERS. Jakob Engstrand... Give me your hand.

ENGSTRAND. *(weeping)* Oh Lord, Sir!

MANDERS. I'm going to give you one last chance.

ENGSTRAND. Oh I beg you to forgive me, sir.

MANDERS. *(embraces him gently)* Perhaps we're both in need of a little forgiveness. I was hard on you.

ENGSTRAND. I needed it, Sir.

MANDERS. If I have misjudged you, then I hope you will not hold it against me.

ENGSTRAND. How could I, Pastor? You have to be cruel only to be kind, as the saying is.

MANDERS. We must start again with a clean slate.

ENGSTRAND. Oh, I hope we can.

MANDERS. What was it you came to tell me?

ENGSTRAND. *(thrown – another moment of panic)* What?

MANDERS. A service in the chapel?

ENGSTRAND. Oh y – yes, Sir –

MANDERS. It would do us both good, I think.

ENGSTRAND. And your advice, Sir. I wanted your advice about the money I've saved. With the work I've been doing here it adds up to quite a lot.

MANDERS. I don't see how I can help.

ENGSTRAND. I've had this idea – it was working on the orphanage made me think of it. I'm hoping to set up a sort of refuge for seamen down in town.

MRS ALVING. *You?*

ENGSTRAND. Yes. It's a busy port – young lads away from home – it's so easy for them to be drawn into temptation. Months at sea, a pocket full of money. What they need is a father figure. Somebody older and wiser that they can look to for help and advice. I know the temptations – I know how to resist them. I could make myself useful.

MANDERS. What do you say to that, Mrs Alving?

ENGSTRAND. I've saved enough to make a start. I'm sure that with your support we could find others what would help us out.

MANDERS. Well, we'll look into it. Now go down to the chapel and tell them to make everything ready. It's getting dark, do you have candles down there?

ENGSTRAND. Oh, yes, Sir. *(takes out his matches and rattles them)*

MANDERS. I'll be down shortly. I think you're in exactly the right frame of mind.

ENGSTRAND. Yes, I believe I am. Good-day, Madam, and thank you? Take care of Regina for me. She's as dear as if she was my own. Maybe dearer. *(exit)*

MANDERS. That was a very different explanation he gave us.

MRS ALVING. It certainly was. *(trying not to laugh)*

MANDERS. You see how careful we must be when judging our fellow men – how easy it is to get the wrong side of the story. Isn't it clear now how that woman duped him? We had no right to assume the worst. Thank God he never knew the whole truth. What's the matter?

MRS ALVING. You're the matter. You're a great baby, Manders, and you always will be!

MANDERS. Me?

MRS ALVING. *(putting her hands on his shoulders)* And I'd like to give you a great big hug!

MANDERS. No, Helen! Good Lord! What are you saying! *(he starts packing the documents into his brief case)* I'd forgotten how demonstrative you can be. So. I'll say good-bye for the moment – I shan't be down there long. And I think you should speak to Osvald when he comes back. Perhaps we've been making too much of it. I can't think he'd be so foolish… *(exit)*

MRS ALVING. *(sighs, looks out of the window at the rain, tidies the room a little. She is about to go into the dining room but stops at the door with a little gasp of surprise)* Osvald? You're still here.

OSVALD. Finishing my cigar.

MRS ALVING. I thought you were going for a walk.

OSVALD. It's too wet. *(a glass clinks.* **MRS ALVING** *sits by the window)* Has Manders gone?

MRS ALVING. He's gone down to the orphanage.

OSVALD. Has he. *(more clinks)*

MRS ALVING. You shouldn't drink so much.

OSVALD. Keeps out the damp.

MRS ALVING. Why don't you come in here?

OSVALD. I'm smoking a cigar.

MRS ALVING. I don't mind cigars.

OSVALD. *(after a pause appears at the door)* Where's Manders?

MRS ALVING. Down at the orphanage. I told you. You shouldn't sit so long at table, Osvald.

OSVALD. Shouldn't I. *(he awkwardly tries to pet her – plays with her hair)* I enjoy just sitting. My mother's home, my mother's dining room – mummy's delicious dinners –

MRS ALVING. No, darling – don't…

OSVALD. *(irritable, paces up and down)* What am I going to do with myself? Can't do any work –

MRS ALVING. Why can't you work?

OSVALD. There's no light. No sun. An artist needs the sun. *(pause)* No – I can't paint here.

MRS ALVING. Perhaps you shouldn't have come home then.

OSVALD. I had to. *(pause)* Had to.

MRS ALVING. Nobody… You know how happy it makes me to have you home – but I'd rather give up my –

OSVALD. Does it make you happy? Do I make you happy?

MRS ALVING. What a question! You're my son.

OSVALD. *(crumpling up a newspaper)* I shouldn't have thought I made much difference to you. You managed pretty well without me all this time.

MRS ALVING. Is that what you think? How can you –

OSVALD. *(silence. It is getting dark.* **OSVALD** *stabs out his cigar)* I've something to tell you. And it's difficult to know how to begin. Let me sit here. *(he sits beside her)* No don't look so –

MRS ALVING. You're frightening me, Osvald. What –

OSVALD. *(he won't look at her)* I've no wish to frighten you but I've got to take you with me – you'll help me shut them out –

MRS ALVING. Who? Shut what out – Osvald?

OSVALD. These fears. I can't free my – mind of fear – my mind. All day yesterday, and today – I've been unable to take a hold on my thoughts – everything rushes through my head – nothing stays –

MRS ALVING. Osvald – *(tries to stand, he pulls her back)*

OSVALD. Just sit still and I'll try to describe it. *(won't look at her)* This exhaustion – this endless depressing exhaustion –

MRS ALVING. It's just the journey –

OSVALD. It is not the journey! Not the journey – *(weeps)*

MRS ALVING. Are you ill?

OSVALD. Look you have to be still and don't interrupt me or I won't be able to go on with it. Be quiet, and calm. I'm not ill in any way you could understand. It's my mind – what's in here won't work anymore. It's drained away, run dry. It's…. gone. I'm finished – empty. *(holds onto her, in tears)*

MRS ALVING. Osvald, stop this! Look at me! listen – It's not true – It's simply not true!

OSVALD. 'Simply not true! Simply not true!' I'm telling you I'm never going to be able to work again. Never. Never. So what am I to do? Sit here with Mother – wasting away – watching the rain?

MRS ALVING. What's happening to you? –

OSVALD. I can't explain – because I don't know how it happened. What have I done? That's what's torturing me. *(pause)* Look… If I'd been degenerate –

MRS ALVING. Osvald –

OSVALD. Leading that sort of life… God this is so difficult. Can you see what I'm trying to say?

MRS ALVING. *(pause)* Yes.

OSVALD. Can you?

MRS ALVING. I –

OSVALD. No. How could you know such a filthy thing? My mother? Do you even know the words? The vile way in which such corruption takes hold? But I never – never have done anything. Never risked anything. Because... I couldn't just... It's not in my nature. I don't...like... Do you believe me?

MRS ALVING. Yes.

OSVALD. It has its claws in my body... and my mind won't focus – everything slips away – runs through my fingers. It never finds a purchase. I've hardly the energy to open my eyes in the morning –

MRS ALVING. You've been overworking – driving yourself too hard.

OSVALD. Yes? I thought so at first. When I was last here – shortly after – when I got back to Paris – I started to get these pains, here, behind the eyes – then here, in the back of my neck, where the spine touches. It feels like an iron ring tightening... here and here.

MRS ALVING. You've always had those headaches – as a child –

OSVALD. Yes – when I was growing up – pains in the head, the joints – severe pains... These are far worse. Last spring I got a commission – a big picture. I couldn't see the canvas – the colours – my imagination deserted me – everything just swam into a blur – and the pain behind my eyes... So. I went to a doctor – one of the best. He told me the truth.

MRS ALVING. What did he say?

OSVALD. He made me describe the symptoms. Then he started asking me all sorts of questions that didn't seem to have anything to do with anything – young men in strange cities – the women they use. But in my case he was way off the mark –

MRS ALVING. Then it can't be what he –

OSVALD. I told him the whole truth. Insisted upon it. He must have thought me a complete innocent. So.

There was, he said, only one other possible explanation. He used a word – vermoulu – do you know what that means?

MRS ALVING. No.

OSVALD. 'Worm-eaten' – riddled with it. He said I must have been riddled with it since birth.

MRS ALVING. With –

OSVALD. With a disease. And I still didn't understand what he was driving at. But then he said... *(anger)* He quoted. 'The sins of the father are visited upon the children' Do you know what he meant by that, Mother? I nearly hit him in the face. *(MRS ALVING walks away)* Do you understand what he was suggesting? So I put him right. My father! Whatever it is could not have been inherited from my father. *(pause)* So everything remains a mystery. In some way I have inflicted an evil upon myself. I cannot imagine how. Why am I being punished? What have I have done that's destroyed me? Is it any wonder I'm driven half mad by it?

MRS ALVING. Oh no...

OSVALD. There's no explanation. I've done nothing – knowingly – wrong. That's why I can't work – can't think. I'm beginning to dream up explanations that I know are not true – and I can no longer distinguish between what I remember and what I dream I remember.

MRS ALVING. No –

OSVALD. My life's as good as over. If I can't work what am I?

MRS ALVING. It can't be true.

OSVALD. Why can't it? Because you don't want it to be? Because you wish it would go away? Sometimes the thought of the pain I cause you seems worse than this real pain. I've tried to persuade myself that you've never cared about me. I thought it might make things easier for us both.

MRS ALVING. You are the only thing in the world... I care about.

OSVALD. I know. When I'm home – with you – I know it. It only increases the pain. *(pause)* Enough – I want to shut it out again – can't discuss it anymore. *(walks away)* Get me something to drink.

MRS ALVING. To drink?

OSVALD. Whatever we have –

MRS ALVING. But, Osvald –

OSVALD. Don't question me! Why can't you make things easy just for once? No more questions! I want to wash these thoughts out of my brain for a while. Do you know another way? *(goes to the window)* Darkness! Silence. This eternal rain – weeks, and months of rain! The sun must despise this place, Mother. *(MRS ALVING pulls the bell rope)* Whenever I come home it's the same. I don't think I've ever seen the sun here.

MRS ALVING. You're going to leave me.

OSVALD. Am I?

MRS ALVING. It's what you're thinking –

OSVALD. I'm finished with thinking.

REGINA. *(coming to the door)* Did you want me?

MRS ALVING. Would you fetch the lamp?

REGINA. Yes, Mrs Alving. I was just going to.

MRS ALVING. Osvald. *(he won't answer)* And fetch us half a bottle of champagne, would you?

REGINA. Yes, Madame. *(exit)*

OSVALD. Thank you, Mother. I'm sorry.

MRS ALVING. You shall have whatever you ask.

OSVALD. I wonder if you mean it. Whatever I ask... You'll give me... give me...

MRS ALVING. Osvald – *(enter REGINA with champagne and two glasses)*

OSVALD. Shh ...

REGINA. Shall I open it?

OSVALD. No. Give it to me. *(REGINA brings in the lamp and puts it on the table. She lights the lamp and the candles in the sconces. It takes a while. A warm glow)*

MRS ALVING. What do you wonder if I mean?

OSVALD. Never mind. Let's have a glass of champagne. *(pours a glass, is about to pour the second)*

MRS ALVING. Thank you. Not for me.

OSVALD. No? *(drinks from his glass and refills it)*

MRS ALVING. Osvald – what did you mean –

OSVALD. Manders was pretty gloomy at lunch – hardly ate a thing. Was it what I said?

MRS ALVING. He hoped you hadn't noticed.

OSVALD. You were quiet too. Manders doesn't look like a priest does he? *(laughs)* It's only when he opens his mouth that the appropriate dryness and sterility leaks out.

MRS ALVING. That's very unfair. He's a good man.

OSVALD. Yes. Tell me about Regina.

MRS ALVING. What about her?

OSVALD. What is she like?

MRS ALVING. In what way?

OSVALD. Mother, you're being obtuse. I find her attractive.

MRS ALVING. You don't know her –

OSVALD. That's why I'm asking about her. Mother?

MRS ALVING. If she'd come to me sooner things might have been different.

OSVALD. What's that supposed to mean?

MRS ALVING. She came from a bad home. She was too long there.

OSVALD. It's not affected her looks.

MRS ALVING. She has faults. Serious faults.

OSVALD. I don't want to hear about them.

MRS ALVING. You asked me to tell you about her. I'm fond of Regina, I feel responsible for her... But she's untrustworthy.

OSVALD. She may be my last hope.

MRS ALVING. Why are you saying these things – you've had too much to drink –

OSVALD. She might be useful – I may need somebody with me –

MRS ALVING. I'm with you!

OSVALD. I know. *(pause)* You are the reason I came home. But you won't do – I can't stay here – I might need to keep Regina by me –

MRS ALVING. Osvald –

OSVALD. I can't rot away in this house! And I don't want you. I don't want you to have to watch it. I have to get away –

MRS ALVING. But you're ill. You don't know what you want. You said it yourself. You don't even know what you're saying.

OSVALD. I could stay... If it were not for the shame. And there's something else I fear – more than anything –

MRS ALVING. What?

OSVALD. Nothing I could tell you. You see? You don't see. That's why you won't do. **(MRS ALVING** *pulls the bell)* Where are you going?

MRS ALVING. I'll show you if I'll do or not! You've nothing to fear. **(REGINA** *comes to the door)* There's nothing wrong with you... Regina fetch another bottle of champagne. Not a half – a whole one this time –

REGINA. Yes, Mrs Alving. *(goes)*

OSVALD. What's all this?

MRS ALVING. The only thing wrong is this house. Life needn't be so dull. It isn't always raining – outside and in.

OSVALD. That girl would balance me. She's a picture of health – I'm falling to bits.

MRS ALVING. Do you wish to discuss her or don't you?

OSVALD. I made her a promise.

MRS ALVING. What promise!

OSVALD. She's always going on about Paris. I said I'd take her some day.

MRS ALVING. What possessed you!

OSVALD. I didn't mean it! But she took me seriously – thinks of nothing else. She's been teaching herself French – can you imagine! I'm afraid she's fallen in love with me. It's a mess!

MRS ALVING. Then she'll just have to fall out of love with you. Paris!

OSVALD. Until I came home this time I've never given her a thought. Now I'm not so sure. She's has so much – *life!* She's what life should be.

MRS ALVING. Oh my son –

(enter REGINA*)*

REGINA. I'm sorry it's taken so long. I had to go down to the cellar.

OSVALD. Fetch another glass.

REGINA. I brought one for Mrs Alving.

OSVALD. For yourself. *(she looks for confirmation to* MRS ALVING*)* Go on!

MRS ALVING. *(cold)* You may join us, Regina. If you wish. *(she goes out for a glass)*

OSVALD. Look how she moves.

MRS ALVING. You can't do this to her, Osvald.

OSVALD. Why can't I? I thought you were going to stop questioning what I say? – 'You can have whatever you want' – isn't that what you told me about half a minute ago? *(*REGINA *comes in with a glass)* Sit down. *(*REGINA *looks at* MRS ALVING *who nods)* Regina – we were discussing the joys of life. *(laughs to himself)* I suspect it's something people in this community don't understand. I've never felt any happiness here.

MRS ALVING. Have I made you unhappy.

OSVALD. You said yourself – it's this house. I'm always unhappy in this house. There's no life in it.

MRS ALVING. You're right. Finally I see it – I'm beginning to understand –

OSVALD. Happiness was my painting. I painted the joyful things my childhood never knew. It's all part of the same thing – happiness, your life's work, and where you find it – how you accomplish it. You don't know what I'm talking about do you?

MRS ALVING. I know more about it than you could imagine.

OSVALD. Up here people say that work's a curse, a punishment. Ask Manders: 'cursed is the ground for thy sake. In sorrow shalt thou eat bread all the days of thy life.'

MRS ALVING. A curse. That's often what we make of it.

OSVALD. In my world nobody will accept that anymore. They tell us 'we're all sinners!' Am I a sinner? I don't think I am. Why should anybody have to carry about the sins of the world on his back? I've not done anything wrong! There are people who think it's wonderful just to be alive. I'm one of them. My work is all about the joy of life. It's what I'm known for. My painting is about light, and sun, and the heat of the south – happiness in fact. The happiness I never knew here. The thought of coming back – being trapped out here – in this graveyard – terrifies me.

MRS ALVING. Terrifies you –

OSVALD. Everything that makes me happy – it's absent here. Any good in me would be poisoned. Ugliness seeps out of the walls. *(she stands up)* What's the matter –

MRS ALVING. I've got something I can tell you now. Both of you.

REGINA. *(standing up)* I think I'd better go.

MRS ALVING. No – I said both of you. Sit down, Regina. It's your turn to help me, Osvald. This is going to be difficult – but I have to speak out. It will be frightening – very frightening for you both – but it's the truth – always the truth! I'm giving you the choice –

MANDERS. *(coming in, wet)* Well, it's still raining out there. But never mind – we've been making good use of the time. I'm sorry. Have I interrupted something important? You know, the more I think about this plan of Engstrand's the more I like the idea. We must give him the chance to reclaim himself. He'll need our support, but it could be the making of him. Ha! Regina will have to help –

REGINA. I couldn't do it, Sir. You can't make me –

MRS ALVING. Regina –

MANDERS. *(who did not notice her when he came in)* What are you doing in here? And with a glass in your hand?

REGINA. *(hastily putting down the glass)* Pardon, M'sieur

OSVALD. She's no concern of yours, Pastor Manders. Regina answers to me from now on. I'm thinking of taking her away from here.

MANDERS. Regina is going nowhere with you, Osvald.

OSVALD. I think you'll find she'll agree. As my wife if that's what she wants.

REGINA. It's nothing to do with me, Sir.

OSVALD. Or if I decide to stay here, she'll stay with me.

REGINA. Stay here?

MANDERS. What have you told them, Helen.

MRS ALVING. I've said nothing yet. But I was about to –

MANDERS. You can't do that –

MRS ALVING. They need the truth. Manders – we all do. *(noises off)*

MANDERS. I forbid you to speak a word until I've had time to advise you privately, Helen.

MRS ALVING. You forbid me! Forbid!

OSVALD. What are you hiding?

REGINA. *(at the window)* Look! What's happening out there? Is it a fire?

OSVALD. A fire? *(going to the window)*

MRS ALVING. *(without looking)* It's the orphanage –

REGINA. It's on fire!

MRS ALVING. Let it burn –

OSVALD. Dear God! The orphanage! My father's orphanage!

MANDERS. It can't be. I've just come from there.

OSVALD. Where's my coat? *(he rushes out)* Aren't you coming for God's sake! It's Father's memorial.

MRS ALVING. Regina, go and get his coat. Osvald! – you must go after him.

MANDERS. It's a judgement!

MRS ALVING. I believe it is –

MANDERS. A judgement on us all –

OSVALD. *(off)* Come on! For God's sake!

MRS ALVING. *(going)* Hurry, Regina –

MANDERS. And we're not insured! *(follows them)*

END OF ACT TWO

ACT THREE

*(**MANDERS** is slumped in a chair unseen by the audience.*
*Enter **REGINA** and **MRS ALVING**)*

REGINA. Still blazing

MRS ALVING. Quite a bonfire.

REGINA. Look! The roof's collapsed – right through into the basement. It'll burn for hours yet.

MRS ALVING. I thought Osvald was following us.

REGINA. I couldn't make him come away.

MRS ALVING. He hasn't even got his coat.

REGINA. Shall I run back with it?

MRS ALVING. No, leave it. I'll fetch him in. He can't do any more down there – nothing left to save *(she goes out into the garden)*

MANDERS. Complete catastrophe! Pray God I don't ever have to live through another night like this one –

REGINA. What I don't understand is how it took hold so quickly. You'd never have though –

MANDERS. Don't go on about it, Regina – I don't want to think about it.

REGINA. But how could a fire have started in there? Who would have –

MANDERS. You too! – Why ask me? Where are all these questions leading! I hope you're not suggesting that I… It's bad enough with Engstrand saying…

REGINA. What? What is he saying?

MANDERS. He's driving me out of my mind –

54

ENGSTRAND. *(calling from the hall)* Pastor Manders! *(enters)*

MANDERS. Dear God! Not here too – he's followed me here!

ENGSTRAND. But what else should I do, Sir? After what's – It's terrible ! – What could you have been thinking of?

MANDERS. I've told you, Engstrand, you're mistaken!

REGINA. What are you talking about?

ENGSTRAND. I blame myself. It was me what persuaded you to come down for the service. If only I'd watched what you were doing – But my head was bowed in prayer.

MANDERS. Engstrand, I assure you –

ENGSTRAND. Nobody else went near them candles – only you, Sir.

MANDERS. So you say. So you say!

ENGSTRAND. Only you –

MANDERS. I don't remember ever having a candle in my hand –

ENGSTRAND. But I saw you, Sir! You snuffed the candle and threw the wick on the floor. There must have been some shavings –

MANDERS. You saw me do it?

ENGSTRAND. I swear, Sir. Bible oath – I watched you –

MANDERS. But I never snuff out altar candles with my fingers – Never –

ENGSTRAND. But I saw you, Sir.

MANDERS. Well I have no memory of doing so. None at all...

ENGSTRAND. What'll happen now?

MANDERS. I need time to think. Can't you leave me alone! *(pause)*

ENGSTRAND. And you hadn't insured it, had you? No insurance! If only you'd insured it before burning it down – no, I'm sorry, that came out wrong – What are you going to do now? – It's a disaster.

MANDERS. Engstrand, please –

ENGSTRAND. The whole town was coming tomorrow – all them poor orphans... It would have been a new life for them. And what about the newspapers – they'll crucify you!

MANDERS. Don't! I shudder to think of it. I'll be pilloried. All the spite – it's not just me that will suffer – they'll use it against the Church – the vilification, the mockery. It will go on, and on – worse than the fire itself.

MRS ALVING. *(coming in)* I can't make him come in. Why so miserable Pastor Manders? Count your blessings. You won't have to stand in the rain tomorrow, making speeches.

MANDERS. I don't know how you can take it so calmly.

MRS ALVING. *(quietly)* It was an act of God. That orphanage was an insult to Him.

MANDERS. You think so?

MRS ALVING. Don't you?

MANDERS. I can take little comfort in the thought.

MRS ALVING. Then look at it only as a business transaction – one that failed. What are you doing here, Engstrand? *(he is in the hall doorway)*

ENGSTRAND. I'm waiting for the Pastor, Ma'am.

MRS ALVING. *(to* **MANDERS***)* Are you going back on the steamer?

MANDERS. There's nothing to stay for now, is there?

MRS ALVING. Take the papers with you. I have to be free of it. There are better things to think of now.

MANDERS. Helen –

MRS ALVING. I'll give you Power of Attorney. Do whatever you judge best.

MANDERS. Well... It's the very least I can do. The original terms of the bequest – The whole document will have to be rewritten.

MRS ALVING. Obviously.

MANDERS. Some good may still come of it. We could make over the Solvik property to the Parish. The rents, and the capital in the bank can be put to good use – The town has plenty of worthy projects crying out for funding.

MRS ALVING. Whatever you think. Just don't involve me.

ENGSTRAND. Don't forget my Home for Sailors, Sir.

MRS ALVING. *(to* MANDERS *who has just been struck by a worse thought)* What is it?

MANDERS. The town is bound to demand an inquiry in to the fire. If Engstrand is right – if it was caused by my negligence – the newspapers won't let me continue with my charitable work. Public opinion will be marshalled to hound me off every committee I serve on.

MRS ALVING. They wouldn't –

MANDERS. They would, Helen. You know they would. I'm the last man to sing my own praises but I have been able to do good – a great deal of good in this community. All that will be finished.

ENGSTRAND. Not if I can help it.

MRS ALVING. I can't believe the town would take the matter so seriously.

MANDERS. Fine sport they'll make of it! They'll throw me to the wolves.

ENGSTRAND. It will never come to that, Sir. I've got a way to put matters right.

MRS ALVING. The worst that could happen is malicious gossip, and some cruel fun at your expense –

MANDERS. You're wrong.

ENGSTRAND. There is a way out, Pastor. I've told you – in one sense I feel it was me what was to blame. If it hadn't been for me you'd never have been down there to set the orphanage ablaze in the first place.

MANDERS. But Engstrand –

ENGSTRAND. I want to repay the trust you've shown in me.

MANDERS. But what are you saying? How...?

ENGSTRAND. It could just as easily have been me what did it. *(pause as it sinks in)*

MANDERS. No – I could never allow that, Jakob. No... Put it out of your mind.

ENGSTRAND. It refuses to go, Sir. I'm good at taking the blame for others. Didn't Our Lord Himself set the example?

MANDERS. Jakob –

ENGSTRAND. Don't do it for yourself. Do it for your charities, for the good of the community – for your calling.

MANDERS. I couldn't. No –

ENGSTRAND. If you think of the people you'll be helping you could.

MANDERS. I... what can I say?

ENGSTRAND. Think of the good what'd come of it. Eveybody would benefit – from the orphans what need your help – more than ever now they haven't got a place of their own, to my lads in the Sailor's Home – everybody.

MANDERS. Dear God, help me – what shall I do!

ENGSTRAND. As you said yourself, Sir, it's not just you – it's what you stand for – the Church. You can't let the papers start having a go at the Church. Whatever next!

MANDERS. You're a good man, Jakob. But I...

ENGSTRAND. I'll come back on the steamer with you, if I may, Sir. You leave it to me. It will come right. Trust me. *(aside to* **REGINA***)* You see how it's done.

MANDERS. I'll get my coat. (**REGINA** *hurries to get it*)

REGINA. It's here.

ENGSTRAND. Yes let's go together. *(to* **REGINA***)* You come home soon, girl. You'll be on the pig's back. *(enter* **OSVALD***)*

REGINA. *(with contempt)* Merci!

MANDERS. Goodbye, Helen. I hope that this house will be free of it's troubles at last. How I regret all that I may have added to them – all.

MRS ALVING. Goodbye, Pastor.

MANDERS. If there is anything I can do to make amends. If ever you need ...

MRS ALVING. Please, no more. You must go.

ENGSTRAND. Goodbye, my child. *(aside)* I've got him! You know where to find me – Little Harbour Street. *(to* **OSVALD***)* Goodbye, Sir. If all goes well with my mission house I shall name it after your dear father – The Captain Alving Sailors' Home. And if I have anything to do with it I can promise you it will be worthy of his memory.

MANDERS. *(at the door)* Yes, yes. Come along then, Jakob. I'm ashamed to think how I've misjudged you... Goodbye, goodbye. *(exit* **MANDERS** *with* **ENGSTRAND***)*

OSVALD. What was Engstrand talking about?

MRS ALVING. It's a project he's discussing with the Pastor... A home for Sailors.

OSVALD. It would burn just like this one.

MRS ALVING. Why do you say that?

OSVALD. Everything burns. I think it's fated. Look at me – I'm burning too. *(***REGINA** *looks frightened)* My father! I've let him down.

MRS ALVING. You're ill. You shouldn't have stayed out there so long.

OSVALD. *(sitting at the table)* You might be right.

MRS ALVING. You're soaked through – frozen. Here... Let me... *(she dries his face with a handkerchief)*

OSVALD. Mother! *(he submits, staring ahead)* Thank you.

MRS ALVING. You must go straight to bed. You need to rest – a good long sleep.

OSVALD. I don't sleep, you know – too scared to sleep.

MRS ALVING. Because you're exhausted – and ill – you're too tired to sleep properly.

REGINA. What's the matter with Mr Alving? Is he –

OSVALD. Shut the doors! Look at me! I'm shaking. With fear!

MRS ALVING. Osvald –

OSVALD. For God's sake, shut the doors –

MRS ALVING. Shut the doors, Regina. *(she does so)* I'll sit with you for a while. *(takes off her outdoor clothes, as does* **REGINA**)

OSVALD. You'll stay with me, won't you, Regina? Yes… She can do whatever's necessary?

REGINA. I'm not sure what you're asking, Mr Alving?

MRS ALVING. I'm your mother, Osvald. And I shall look after you.

OSVALD. *(smiles)* You wouldn't have the courage, Mother. *(stares at her)* Though I suppose you'd have the right – you brought me into the world… it would be only fitting.

MRS ALVING. What are you saying?

OSVALD. I wish you'd stop being so formal with me, Regina. Call me Osvald.

REGINA. Mrs Alving wouldn't like it.

MRS ALVING. Perhaps you should be on first name terms. When you hear what I have to say… Come and sit down with us. (**REGINA** *hesitates, confused)* Come on. *(she does so)* Osvald, I'm going to tell you something that will take away your fear – put an end to the guilt, the worry of it all…

OSVALD. If only you could.

MRS ALVING. I'm your mother. I have that power.

OSVALD. Don't raise my hopes –

MRS ALVING. When you spoke about the joy of life – the joy that should be in life, I looked back on what my own has been, and what it should have been.
I wish you could have known your father – when he was a young man. He understood it all.

OSVALD. I know he did.

MRS ALVING. He seemed like the force of life itself – immortal, powerful – he had such spirit! If you had heard him laugh... Oh, everybody thought the sun shone out of him!

OSVALD. It did.

MRS ALVING. And then this boy – that's all he ever was – a boy – came to live here in this bleak, grey town – full of dead souls – where hypocrisy silences every generous impulse, and the only pleasures are vicious.

His life here was without purpose. There was no great work, no challenge. Just the clock ticking away... The rain. No love to consume him. That's all there was for him. For us.

OSVALD. Mother –

MRS ALVING. What happened was inevitable –

OSVALD. What –

MRS ALVING. You said it yourself – what would happen to you if you stayed here – wasting away – watching the rain. A death in life –

OSVALD. And my father?

MRS ALVING. I could do nothing for him – I helped destroy him. I was a girl when we married. They'd taught me about duty – how to behave – get on in the right circles – respectable, narrow-minded circles – what to think – what was acceptable – My duty. His duty. And I believed it! The truth is, Osvald, that – quite innocently – I made your father's life unbearable – and he had no escape from it in his own home – from me.

OSVALD. I don't believe you.

MRS ALVING. The joy of living died in him. He was a tiger in a cage. And I could do nothing to help him – I brought no sunshine into his life. *(pause)* Your father drank – he was a lecher – and that had its consequences.

OSVALD. Why are you making up such stories? If they were true you'd have told me before now. I'd have known.

MRS ALVING. In the past I saw things differently – right up until this moment –

OSVALD. How did you see things?

MRS ALVING. Alving was a broken man – a ruin – even before you were born. What you knew of him came from me – every week while you were away – a letter. I invented for you, a father any boy could be proud of.

OSVALD. *(softly)* Did you. *(he gets up and goes to the window)*

MRS ALVING. I have been hiding a terrible truth. That Regina should have the same rights in this house as my own son.

REGINA. I should...?

MRS ALVING. Yes.

REGINA. *(it sinks in)* My mother was a whore then?

MRS ALVING. That's harsh –

REGINA. It's the right word for it, isn't it? I don't remember much about her but there've been times when the thought's crossed my mind... that she was like that. Engstrand's wife. *(thinks)* I shall have to leave. Probably best if I go right away, don't you think?

MRS ALVING. Do you want to go?

REGINA. It's for the best.

MRS ALVING. Whatever you wish.

OSVALD. What are you talking about! She's not leaving. This is her home – more than ever now. Regina? *(going to her)*

REGINA. Thank you, Sir...

MRS ALVING. I've not been fair to you, Regina –

REGINA. You haven't, have you? Doesn't matter. You're not much of a prospect are you, Osvald? I can't see myself as a nursemaid for sick little boys – here nor at the orphanage. But of course that's gone too. I suppose it was Engstrand who burned it down – trust him for that! What a terrible place this is!

OSVALD. But now that you know how close we really are –

REGINA. Close? How do I feel about that? There's nothing –
no sisterly feeling at all. Sorry. All the time I've wasted
out here! I've got a lot of catching up to do. When it
comes to the joy of life, Madame, I've got plenty.

MRS ALVING. I'm afraid you have. But don't throw yourself
away, Regina.

REGINA. If Osvald takes after our father I expect I'm like
my mother. But it's not really up to me is it? It's the
way we're made. May I ask, Madame, how much Pastor
Manders knows?

MRS ALVING. Everything.

REGINA. I'll go back with them on the steamer. I better
hurry. Did you see the way Engstrand twists him round
his little finger? I ought to be as good at it as he is.
If there's money coming to him I ought to have my
share.

MRS ALVING. You're welcome to it, Regina.

REGINA. *(with a hard look at her)*
No you didn't play fair with me. If I'd had my rights
you'd have brought me up as a gentleman's daughter –
you should have made a lady of me. Now I can only
be what I am. Oh well, who cares! It might be fun.
Champagne, champagne all the way!

MRS ALVING. When you've thought things through... You
know there will always be a home for you here.

OSVALD. Regina –

REGINA. A home! A home? I'd be better off in an institution!
No thanks. I'll try my luck with Pastor Manders. If I
can't get anything out of him, there's one place I know
where I'll always get a welcome.

MRS ALVING. Where?

REGINA. The Captain Alving Memorial Home for naughty
sailor boys. I shall be about my father's business – one
way or another.

MRS ALVING. I can imagine what will happen to you.

REGINA. I don't know about that. But what a time I'll have finding out! *(exit)* Adieu, Madame – Monsieur!

OSVALD. You should have made her stay.

MRS ALVING. This has been a terrible ordeal for you –

OSVALD. About my father you mean?

MRS ALVING. Well of course.

OSVALD. I can't see that it matters.

MRS ALVING. But it should matter. Your father was utterly wretched –

OSVALD. Well I'm sorry for him – who wouldn't be. But...

MRS ALVING. He was your father, Osvald!

OSVALD. Oh, 'my father! My father!' All I ever knew of him was a lie you invented for me. A lie that's lasted my whole lifetime. My only truthful memory of my father is that once, quite deliberately, he made me sick.

MRS ALVING. That's a terrible thing to say! It's natural that a son should feel more than that for a father –

OSVALD. Is it? What do I have to thank him for? A name – a wasting disease. I can't manufacture love for a man who was, and remains, a stranger to me. What love does Regina feel for her brother? It's just romantic nonsense –

MRS ALVING. Romantic nonsense?

OSVALD. Long lost parents – the power of love – it's the stuff of plays and housemaids' novels. It's not real life.

MRS ALVING. *(troubled)* Ghosts... I can hear you father's voice.

OSVALD. You might well call us ghosts.

MRS ALVING. Perhaps you can't love me either?

OSVALD. At least I know you.

MRS ALVING. Is that all you feel?

OSVALD. What do I feel? *(pause)* Now that I'm ill...

MRS ALVING. You need my love, Osvald. This disease has brought you home to me. We can make some good of that. I can see that you're not mine yet, but I can win you back.

OSVALD. That's just words. I'm sick, Mother. From now on I shall have to be thinking about myself. I don't know that there'll be much room for anyone else.

MRS ALVING. I won't ask much of you.

OSVALD. *(laughs)* I'll expect you to be cheerful – a good companion.

MRS ALVING. I can try! At least I've taken the guilt of it away. You don't have to reproach yourself for anything.

OSVALD. Now take away the terror.

MRS ALVING. The terror?

OSVALD. That's something Regina would have done.

MRS ALVING. Regina?

OSVALD. How late is it?

MRS ALVING. Almost morning. *(looking out)* I think we're going to have a fine day for once. The sun will be coming up over the hills.

OSVALD. Well that's something. Perhaps there'll be other things to be glad of – to make me want to hold on to life –

MRS ALVING. I know there will –

OSVALD. Even if I can't ever work again.

MRS ALVING. But, Osvald, how do you know that? I think you will work – now that the guilt has gone – now that you don't have to torture yourself – going over and over... Your painting will be part of the cure...

OSVALD. The cure?

MRS ALVING. It will be something to build on – to make you happy.

OSVALD. The cure! God!... Mother, there is no cure. There is no cure! Now come over here. I'll tell you what you're going to do for me. Then the sun will come out. And this terror I have will...

MRS ALVING. I'll do anything you ask.

OSVALD. Good. You promised to give me whatever I wanted.

MRS ALVING. And I meant it, Osvald –

OSVALD. Nothing in the world you wouldn't do for me.

MRS ALVING. That was my promise.

OSVALD. But do you understand your promise?

MRS ALVING. Osvald, you're all I have left in the world – all I have to live for.

OSVALD. Yes. Perhaps you could be strong.

MRS ALVING. I am strong –

OSVALD. I'm not sure I can say the words.

MRS ALVING. What could be more terrible than all I've suffered? I am strong, Osvald.

OSVALD. You won't make a scene, or scream, or do any of those things that – you'll just sit quietly and listen? Promise me.

MRS ALVING. Yes, yes. But –

OSVALD. It's not the exhaustion. It's not my inability to work that terrifies me. It's not even the guilt. It's the nature of this disease – how it takes hold… What happens – what will happen… *(points at his head)* It starts in here. In the brain –

MRS ALVING. Oh don't! Oh God!

OSVALD. You promised you'd listen. It's deep inside my brain – waiting to begin the work of corruption. It may happen any day – at any minute –

MRS ALVING. Oh my son !

OSVALD. Be my loving mother –

MRS ALVING. It's too cruel –

OSVALD. It is. I've had one attack already – in Paris. Didn't last long. There was no pain. But when I found out what it had done to me… what had been happening inside my body – that's when I knew what the end would be like – and the terror got its claws into me. That's why I came home.

MRS ALVING. Then it's fear of –

OSVALD. I'm not afraid to die. But when you think of
death you think – you hope – it will be peaceful,
clean – drifting away... My death will be loathesome –
unspeakable... Something I can't face.

MRS ALVING. Don't say any more now. I need to think – to
breathe –

OSVALD. A parody of childhood. To be fed – washed – but
not a child's body – healthy, growing –

MRS ALVING. Osvald stop!

OSVALD. To be trapped inside a man's body – my
body – decaying, rotting –

(He dissolves into tears)

MRS ALVING. I am your Mother. Who else should nurse
you –

OSVALD. No! Not that! *(on his feet)* I don't want that. *(calm
again)* I daren't think that I might go on like that for
years and years – I could outlive you – that's what the
doctor told me. *(he sits by her)* He called it a softening
of the brain – or something like that. *(smiles)* At the
time I rather liked the expression he used – it made
me think of cherry velvet curtains – something soft
that you could stroke –

MRS ALVING. *(convulsed)* Osvald!

OSVALD. Why did you have to frighten Regina away? If only
I'd been able to keep her – she'd have given me what
I need.

MRS ALVING. I've told you. I can give you anything you
need.

OSVALD. Well, then... The doctor said that the next attack
will finish me. When it comes – and it will come –
there'll be no more hope.

MRS ALVING. That was callous of him. What do doctors
know –

OSVALD. Oh, he knew. I made him spell it out. I needed
all the details. So I could make arrangements. *(smiles)*
Look, Mother.

MRS ALVING. What is it?

OSVALD. Morphia.

MRS ALVING. Oh, Osvald – my son!

OSVALD. Twelve tablets. More than enough –

MRS ALVING. Give them to me! *(snatching)* Osvald! Don't even think of it!

OSVALD. No not yet. There's no need… *(puts it back in his pocket)*

MRS ALVING. I withdraw my… I could never do it.

OSVALD. But you must. There's nobody else now. If Regina had been here she'd have done what I asked.

MRS ALVING. She couldn't –

OSVALD. When she saw me lying there, in terror, helpless, past all hope –

MRS ALVING. She would never have done it. She hasn't the strength –

OSVALD. When she realised what she'd got – that carefree, stupid girl – she'd have put me down like a sick animal.

MRS ALVING. Then thank God she has gone.

OSVALD. *(puts the pill box on the table)* So now you know – what you must do.

MRS ALVING. *(horrified)* I?

OSVALD. Who better?

MRS ALVING. Your mother?

OSVALD. Because you're my mother.

MRS ALVING. I gave you life!

OSVALD. Take it back…

MRS ALVING. Help. Help. We must get help –

OSVALD. Where are you going? Don't leave me. There is no help –

MRS ALVING. A doctor. The best doctors – *(she goes out, he follows her)*

OSVALD. You're not going anywhere! *(a key is turned, she comes back)* And nobody is coming in.

MRS ALVING. Osvald, Osvald –

OSVALD. I can't be at peace with myself until I'm sure of you. What sort of mother's love keeps me suffering like this?

MRS ALVING. My son –

OSVALD. What sort of love?

MRS ALVING. *(forcing herself)* I'll do whatever you ask. *(they embrace for a long time)* If it ever becomes necessary. When the time comes – if it does. But it won't. It won't. Life's never that unkind.

OSVALD. We'll be together for as long as we can. Thank you. Thank you, Mother. I'm calm now.

MRS ALVING. Are you?

OSVALD. Yes.

MRS ALVING. Think of it as a bad dream. Just a bad dream. All those months of pain and worry… with nobody to comfort you. The fear just grew and grew and you had nobody to take it away. But now your mother's with you. You're home and you're safe and you'll have a good long rest. My darling. I'll give you everything you ask – just as I did when you were a little boy. Osvald. My little boy. There! You're better now. It's all over – the nightmare's gone. *(she goes to the window)* You see how simple it was – what did I tell you? And look at the sun. Brilliant sunshine! Isn't that what you wanted? Now you'll really be able to see your home.

(The morning sun is shining through the window; she goes to the table and puts out the lamp)

OSVALD. *(sitting motionless with his back to the window)* Mother. Give me the sun.

MRS ALVING. *(at the table)* What did you say?

OSVALD. *(without expression)* The sun… the sun …

MRS ALVING. Osvald… What's the matter? *(he seems to shrink; muscles relax; face without expression; eyes stare ahead)* What is it? Osvald – tell me – what's happening to you? Osvald! Osvald look at me.

OSVALD. the sun… the sun…

MRS ALVING. Oh God! No, no, no – my child, my beautiful
   boy, *(she takes the box)* Dear God, no – *(she holds him,
   nodding "yes, yes, yes")*
OSVALD. Give me the sun...
   (The lights grow and grow into a brilliant white light)

END

Lightning Source UK Ltd.
Milton Keynes UK
UKOW05f0710290914

239342UK00001B/14/P